Arabesque

Arabesque

Narrative Structure and the Aesthetics
of Repetition in the *1001 Nights*

SANDRA NADDAFF

Northwestern University Press
Evanston, Illinois

Northwestern University Press
Evanston, Illinois 60201

Library of Congress Cataloging-in-Publication Data

Naddaff, Sandra.
    Arabesque : narrative structure and the aesthetics of repetition
in the 1001 nights / Sandra Naddaff.
      p. cm.
    Includes bibliographical references and index.
    ISBN 0-8101-0976-X. — ISBN 0-8101-0990-5 (pbk.)
    1. Arabian nights—Style. 2. Repetition in literature.
I. Title.
PJ7731.N34   1991
398.22—dc20   91-10102
                                                                     CIP

To my parents
and
To Leigh

Contents

Contents

Acknowledgments

So many people have contributed to this book in so many different ways that it is not possible to thank each of them individually. Let me say at the outset, then, how very grateful I am to the many friends, colleagues, and students who have helped me as I've gone along.

Virginia Woolf's room of one's own and five hundred pounds are still notoriously difficult for a woman in academe to find. I wish particularly to thank those foundations who, both practically and symbolically, have provided me with those valuable commodities. The American Association of University Women awarded me the Palmer Fellowship in 1986–87 for research work not directly associated with this book, but important, nonetheless, for the way in which it influenced my thinking about the *1001 Nights*. Similarly, among other things, the funding generously provided by the Lurcy Charitable and Education Trust in 1990–91 allowed me to prepare this manuscript for publication.

Equally important, though, has been the encouragement of those who have simultaneously served as friends, colleagues, and teachers. Muhsin Mahdi and Claudio Guillén were wise and supportive advisors while *Arabesque* was living its life as a dissertation, and beyond. Since then, I have been lucky enough to work with equally wise and generous colleagues in literature at Harvard. Chris Braider, Dorrit Cohn, Greg Nagy, David Perkins, and Jurij Striedter have provided the kind of intellectual and personal support that has made all the difference to me. I thank them all for their many kindnesses.

Carol Cross helped greatly in the preparation of the notes of *Arabesque*. Denise Wise offered much moral and practical support. Ruth Melville's copyediting skills were indispensable. Ramona Naddaff was the best kind of proofreader anyone could hope to have. And Susan Harris of Northwestern University Press made the process of making the manuscript a book thoroughly pleasurable. I would also like to thank Jonathan Brent, formerly of Northwestern University Press, for his initial encouragement and support of this project.

I have often thought that one of the hidden lessons of the *1001 Nights* is the importance of family. From her father, the wazir, who provokes Shahrazad into action, to her sister, Dunyazad, who is instrumental in carrying out Shahrazad's plot, to her children who are in a sense the end result of her thousand and one nights of storytelling, family plays a significant role in the unfolding of the *1001 Nights*. My own family has been equally significant in the making of *Arabesque*. My mother and father have given so often in so many different ways that I would need a thousand and one nights of my own to thank them for everything they've done. My various siblings have generously donated their time and counsel. And my sons, Nathaniel and Benjamin, have from the beginning reminded me of just what's important in our lives. But it is my husband and friend, Leigh Hafrey, who deserves the greatest credit in all this. For all the times he has urged, encouraged, and loved, I thank him.

Cambridge, Mass.
August 1991

Arabesque

Chapter One

Flexible Borders and Mutable Texts

A wise man has said: "Writing is a spiritual geometry wrought by a material instrument."
—al-Āmulī, *Nafāʾis al-Funūn*

The case with them (viz. some legendary stories) is similar to that of the books that have come to us from the Persian, Indian, and the Greek and have been translated for us, and that originated in the way that we have described, such as for example the book *Hazār Afsāna,* which in Arabic means "thousand tales," for "tale" is in Persian *afsāna.* The people call this book "Thousand Nights." This is the story of the king and the vizier and his daughter and her servant girl; these two are called Shīrazād and Dīnāzād.[1]

So runs the earliest known extended reference to the work entitled *Alf Laylah wa-Laylah,* the *1001 Nights.* It is a work that, like most works deriving from an oral folk source, possesses no fixed or privileged textual identity. From its Persian incarnation recalled above by the Arab historian al-Masʿūdī in A.D. 947 to its early eighteenth-century embodiment in

Antoine Galland's famous translation as *Les mille et une nuits: Contes arabes*, from its Grub Street dubbing as the *Arabian Nights* to its first appearance as a "complete" printed Arabic text in 1835, the *1001 Nights* has spoken both of the difficult metamorphosis from oral to written text and, perhaps even more eloquently, of the forced translation from East to West.

The result is an unusually long and complicated literary and textual history. As with all works of popular and folk literature, one cannot locate the origins of the collection of stories we call the *1001 Nights;* indeed, once the transmission from oral to written has been made (and there is evidence that a manuscript of *Alf Laylah* existed as early as the ninth century), one cannot even accurately speak of *the* fixed text of the *1001 Nights.* One is instead confronted with a multiplicity of editions, ranging from the so-called first Calcutta edition of only the first two hundred nights (vol. 1, 1814; vol. 2, 1818); to the Breslau edition spuriously claimed to be based on a Tunisian manuscript (1824–43); followed by the famous Bulaq edition of 1835, noted by the scholar Duncan Black MacDonald in his classic *Encyclopaedia Brittannica* article to have the dignity of a vulgate; up through the second Calcutta edition, published in four volumes in 1839–42.[2]

The most recent edition of *Alf Laylah* proves also to be the definitive one.[3] Based on a fourteenth-century Syrian manuscript meticulously edited by Muhsin Mahdi, this edition is the first to have received careful scholarly attention. This Syrian manuscript is the oldest one extant; like the other manuscripts of *Alf Laylah* derived from this branch, it contains only 282 nights. Mahdi has made the corrections and emendations necessary for a scholarly edition, while at the same time allowing the text to preserve its original oral flavor. In short, he has refrained from forcing the text to assume a "literary" guise as every past editor has done, and in so doing has brought into being a kind of urtext of *Alf Laylah.* This edition promises to be the one on which all future studies of the *1001 Nights* will be based, thereby replacing the earlier "classic" Bulaq edition. It is this new edition that has supported the present study.

The history of both the manuscripts and the editions of the *1001 Nights* has been discussed at length by scholars over the past century. Duncan Black MacDonald and Muhsin Mahdi, in particular, have exhaustively analyzed both the different manuscript families from which the printed versions of the *Nights* derive and the history of the editions that have ensued.[4] What the subtext of this history tells of most interestingly is that this originally oral popular narrative has, perhaps more than other works in the same category, been subject to innumerable transformations and metamorphoses. The text of the *1001 Nights* possesses no fixed boundaries beyond the limits of its frame story. Although certain story cycles recur in all recensions of the *Nights* (e.g., "The Story of the Merchant and the Jinni," "The Story of the Porter and the Three Ladies," "The Story of the Hunchback"), they alone do not constitute the sine qua non of *Alf Laylah*. To a large extent, the metamorphic value of this text is due to its original status as oral folklore, and the consequent circumstances of its performance and transmission. But I would suggest that the *1001 Nights* is particularly prone to textual transformation, that its boundaries are particularly flexible, its content, its language, particularly malleable even after it is "fixed" in print, for two reasons.

The first has to do with the essential fact that the all-important narrator of the *1001 Nights* tales themselves is a woman. (The frame story is, of course, narrated in a different voice.) Shahrazad is characterized by nothing if not her fertility—both narrative and otherwise—and it is a tribute to her legacy of potentially infinite narrative generation that the text possesses an ability, indeed a willingness, to accommodate ultimately any tale between its ever-flexible borders, in the interests of maintaining narrative variety. The second issue at hand is to some extent poised in counterbalance to this fact. No work of Arabic or even Islamic literature is as well known to the Western world as the *1001 Nights*. No text has been so completely appropriated, remade, refigured, both literally and rhetorically, by its translators as the *1001 Nights*, the *Arabian Nights, The Thousand Nights and a Night*. Jorge Luis Borges's now classic article on the translators of the *1001 Nights* bears witness to the strong desire of any translator of this text to rewrite it in his own image (and all translators of *Alf Laylah* have up to now been men).[5] This is something that could perhaps have been accomplished only with greater difficulty if the narrator were not, of necessity, so pliable, so accommodating, so fertile. As it stands, Shahrazad's narrative expansiveness knows no bounds even when it comes to crossing the literary, cultural, and political borders between East and West.

Nothing speaks so eloquently to this as Galland's re-creation of *Alf Laylah*. Faced with a truncated manuscript and a number of nights far short of the necessary thousand and one, Galland tapped Hanna Diab, a Syrian man of his acquaintance, who provided his own oral rendition of various tales of the *1001 Nights* variety which Galland in turn outlined and rewrote for inclusion in his translated text. When even this human source ran dry, Galland searched the libraries of Europe for isolated Arabic manuscripts of suitable tales in order to acquire the requisite number of nights. There is a certain irony in the fact that the work that launched the tremendous vogue of the *conte orientale* and introduced the *1001 Nights* to Europe was, in some sense, textually illegitimate. And there is a further irony in the fact that those cycles that are best known today and that are thought of as quintessentially *1001 Nights* material, cycles such as "Sindbad the Sailor" and "The Story of Aladdin and the Magic Lamp," are not part of the original Arabic corpus of tales.

This textual mutability and malleability continue today. As recently as 1985 the Egyptian government confiscated a new, unexpurgated rendition of the *1001 Nights* and allowed only a censored, Islamically "correct" version of the text to be sold. And yet *Alf Laylah* persists as one of our fundamental examples of narrative art, precisely because of the work's ability to accommodate so graciously any tale within its all-encompassing frame. But the degree to which the text has been repeatedly rewritten and refashioned also speaks to the narrative art of infinite variation and re-creation which Shahrazad so artfully manipulates in order to sway the king through her storytelling powers.

This study limits itself to an examination of one specific cycle within the *1001 Nights* corpus. Precisely because of the enormous narrative variety embraced by the frame tale of *Alf Laylah,* the exercise of speaking about the *1001 Nights* as an entity quickly becomes futile. A study such as Ferial Ghazoul's *The Arabian Nights: A Structural Analysis* expertly avoids the problem of generalization by looking at the way the frame story influences each tale that filters through it. But except for Ghazoul's book and the general introductory work by Mia Gerhardt, studies that focus on a particular cycle or cycles have been more successful in giving the reader a sense of the texture and technique of this paragon of narrative art.[6]

"The Story of the Porter and the Three Ladies" is a particularly rich cycle on which to focus, in part because it is present in a relatively stable form in all recensions regardless of date and origin. This suggests a story cycle that was already well developed and coherent before it was fixed in literary form, which allows the reader to make more easily certain assumptions and deductions about both its narrative form and the larger narrative of which it is a part. But it is also an important cycle to study because it is undoubtedly one of the most complicated of the *1001 Nights* narratives. Like those other cycles that are instigated solely by the act of storytelling, "The Story of the Hunchback," for example, or "Sindbad," "The Story of the Porter and the Three Ladies" consists of a frame story within which unroll at all levels of narrative remove the tales of its main characters. In this it is unlike such companion pieces as "The Story of the Three Apples" or "The Story of Nur al-Din Ali ibn Bakkar and the Slave Girl Shams al-Nahar," cycles in which the presence of narrative-men and -women (Todorov's *hommes-récits*) and the consequent narrative act is limited. Storytelling is, in fact, the main activity of "The Porter and the Three Ladies." Although the characters fall in love, die, are transformed from humans into animals, and journey to faraway places, it is ultimately only the narrative act, the ability to tell about these various experiences, that has value within this particular narrative universe. Indeed, with the exception perhaps of the Hunchback's tale, no other cycle provides so many levels of narrative embedding, so many tales within tales. In this, the series mirrors the original frame story of the larger work within which it is itself embedded. In both narrative and thematic terms, "The Porter and the Three Ladies" speaks of its progenitrix, the tale of Shahrazad, and amplifies the larger narrative issues sketched before the first of the 1001 Nights begins.

But it is not only in its acrobatic manipulation of the narrative act that "The Porter and the Three Ladies" imitates the frame story—something the two brief cycles that intervene between it and the tale of Shahrazad do as well, albeit to a far less complicated degree. "The Porter and the Three Ladies" is an important cycle to examine for the way in which it reenacts the sexual tensions inaugurated in the frame story. As I will argue in the following chapter, "The Porter and the Three Ladies" is premised upon a kind of gendered opposition. The initial tension in this cycle between male and female develops into an opposition between different kinds of discourse and, consequently, different ways of viewing the world; and in this, again, the cycle develops the all-important connection between the sexual and the textual initiated in the frame story. It is because of such correspondences and their subsequent complication and elaboration that "The Story of the Porter and the Three Ladies" becomes a particularly important cycle to examine. Again, this is not to say that the mechanisms of narrative and the issues of gender raised by this cycle are present in every cycle of the *1001 Nights* as a whole, for not every cycle operates according to the constraints and concerns apparent in this one. But given its close narrative connection to Shahrazad's tale (as well as its relatively close proximity), we can't help feeling that the narrative concerns and tendencies exhibited in their most complicated form by this cycle are particularly significant. If a careful examination of "The Porter and the Three Ladies" doesn't provide us with a kind of all-purpose guide to the *1001 Nights,* it can at least provide us with a detailed road map of the territory covered by this Baghdadian porter and his three female companions. As it happens, this is territory inhabited by other narratively generated cycles within the text as well.

My aim here is to isolate and explain these narrative concerns and tendencies, to define the basic narrative development of this particular cycle, to understand why "The Porter and the Three Ladies" undercuts those expectations surrounding narrative structure and plot development which we typically bring to our reading of narratives and which are indeed met in other cycles within the *1001 Nights* itself. Why does reading this and other cycles premised upon the act of narration resemble more the descent into an underground cave (a space that figures prominently in these tales) rather than the journey along a road, however winding (a cycle like "Qamar al-Zaman," for example)? How does the presence of women in these narratives influence this descent? Why does the narrative move backward to a time preceding its opening rather than into the future in order to arrive at its conclusion? Why do the individual tales repeat almost obsessively themes, motifs, characters, and actions both within and without their immediate purview? These are issues that have significance within a larger literary theoretical context; indeed one of the interests of a cycle like "The Porter and the Three Ladies" is that in its own insistent narrative self-reflection, it easily opens up, almost seems to demand, a dialogue with issues of narrative theory, and thereby allows the possibility of an interface between the narrative itself on the one hand and a kind of theoretical questioning on the other. What one hopes to come away with is not only a new narrative context for thinking about issues of narrative development but a larger theoretical context within which to think about narratively generated, self-referential cycles of "The Porter and Three Ladies" kind within the *Nights* as a whole.

Although the status of the *1001 Nights* as a work of folk or popular narrative is certainly important to an understanding of the work, it is not to the particular questions and concerns of folk literature per se that I wish to address myself. Those questions of folk literary creation, transmission, and performance, while interesting and important, are, for my purposes, subsumed into the larger issues of narrative structure and development addressed in this study. Issues revolving around the role of narrative repetition, for example, or the function of the narrator or storyteller within a particular society, though foregrounded in folk texts, are not limited to them and can offer significant insight into issues of narrative development and technique in later, fixed texts. The further reaches of my examination extend to the function of metaphor as a trope that helps to engender narrative as well as to the function of repetition as a mode of narrative development. The final attempt of this study is to interpret these functions in the light of the development of the Islamic ornament of arabesque, to explore the way in which the aesthetic behind the arabesque and its pattern of development offers us another way of understanding how and why such cycles as "The Porter and the Three Ladies" within (and perhaps without) the *Nights* develop. This is not an effort to locate the *1001 Nights* within a limited, culturally defined tradition, though the fact that "The Porter and the Three Ladies" grows up in the same cultural environment as that of the arabesque is certainly suggestive, if not necessary. It is rather an attempt to unravel the intricately woven threads of a text that tells about the way that narrative is made in the closed, privileged, perhaps even rarefied space of the three ladies and other cycles in which the act of narration is insisted upon. That such narratives continue to be made outside this particular space, and potentially even beyond the limits of this text, is all to our advantage.

I have benefited from much prior work on both the *1001 Nights* and narrative theory. Andras Hamori, in *On the Art of Medieval Arabic Literature* and numerous articles, has beautifully explored the workings of individual story cycles within the *Nights* with an eye to both their narrative underpinnings and their literary historical context. In a critical study pivoting around the extended cycle of "Ajib and Gharib," André Miquel offers a masterful reading of one particular cycle of the *1001 Nights*, bringing to the fore its distinguishing narrative features and characteristics—an approach he brings to bear with equal success in *Sept contes des "Mille et une nuits."*[7] And the above-cited work of Ferial Ghazoul, *The Arabian Nights: A Structural Analysis,* provides a broad overview of the way the text as a whole is put together and expertly foregrounds some of the issues that I focus on in my reading of "The Porter and the Three Ladies"—for example, the metaphoric nature of what she terms the "matricial phrase," the structuring principle of binarism, the ensuing patterns of repetition. Whereas Ghazoul is concerned with these issues as larger structuring devices for the *Nights* as a complete text, however, I prefer to develop these issues more closely with an eye to reading a specific kind of cycle in the *1001 Nights.*[8]

Similarly, the theoretical context on which this study

draws has already been established by structuralist and poststructuralist critics alike. I have tried in my analysis to draw on those texts that have already achieved classic status. An early essay such as Tzvetan Todorov's "Les hommes-récits," for example, expertly constructs the scaffolding that supports a larger reading of the all-important embedding/embedded narrative that the *1001 Nights* best represents.[9] Similarly, certain fundamental, now canonic texts dealing with basic narratological issues (Jakobson, Todorov, Genette) and others dealing more particularly with the status of repetition both as a literary and a philosophic element (Brooks, Miller, Deleuze) have provided useful support to my own exploration of the narrative complications at hand.[10] What we ultimately hope to accomplish in such an investigation is yet a further understanding of why narrative can work such a powerful spell. It is in medieval Baghdad with three ladies and a porter that we can begin.

Chapter Two

Magic Words
Metaphoric Initiation

But the greatest thing by far is to be a maker of metaphor. It is the one thing that can not be learned from others; and it is also a sign of genius, since a good metaphor implies an intuitive perception of the similarity in dissimilars.
—Aristotle, *Poetics*

... la danseuse *n'est pas une femme qui danse,* pour ces motifs juxtaposés qu'elle *n'est pas une femme,* mais une métaphore résumant un des aspects élémentaires de notre forme, glaive, coupe, fleur, etc., et qu'*elle ne danse pas,* suggérant, par le prodige de raccourcis ou d'élans, avec une écriture corporelle ce qu'il faudrait des paragraphes en prose dialoguée autant que descriptive, pour exprimer, dans la rédaction: poëme dégagé de tout appareil du scribe.
—Mallarmé, *Crayonné au théâtre*

I

THE labyrinthine tribute to Kufic calligraphy that stands as the frontispiece to Richard Burton's monumental translation of the *1001 Nights* offers an eloquent interpretation of the fundamental meaning of the work.[1] For as contemporary critics have remarked, the *1001 Nights* is essentially a story about telling stories, a work that is initially generated and ultimately sustained by the narrative act.[2] In the process of unfolding, it reflects back upon itself, mirrors itself, indeed tells about itself and about narrative in general. In so doing, it asserts itself as a treatise on the basic elements of narrative and explores the function of the word and its status as the generative force behind the text. Just as *kitāb*, "book," initiates Burton's calligram and thereby engenders the scriptive structure (the word *kitāb* sits in every corner of the Kufic square followed by *Alf Laylah*, "Thousand Nights"; the center is filled by calligraphic variations on the phrase), so is the book in turn engendered by the word that begins the tale of Shahrazad's first night: *za'amū*, "they claim," or, as Husain Haddawy translates it, "it is said."

The other important fact about the *1001 Nights* is that, with the exception of the important opening and closing frames of the text (which set up the initial narrative situation regarding King Shahrayar and provide the necessary closure to Shahrazad's story), the dominant, enframing narrative voice is that of a woman. It is Shahrazad, beguilingly intelligent, narratively proficient and prolific, who is the supreme storyteller in this text and the ventriloquist who manipulates the varied voices of the characters whose stories she tells. It is she who seemingly determines both the narrative and the sexual context by means of which she reeducates or, perhaps more accurately, reindoctrinates the king; and it is she who, by means of her narrative and sexual powers, saves womankind from violent extinction. The question one ends up asking over and over again, though, is how does Shahrazad do this? What is it that finally makes her tales so distinctive, so powerful, so redemptive? Why is it that the tales told by Shahrazad in the *1001 Nights* are ultimately awarded that highest of textual honors in this universe: no longer to be orally conveyed but to be transfixed forever in gold ink?

As if in partial answer to this question, the verbal form *balaghanī*, "it has reached me," which alternates with *za'amū* in opening Shahrazad's tales, is directly related to the noun *balāghah*, the term used in classical Arabic poetics for rhetoric; and indeed, the generative power of the word is not strictly limited to its narrative consequences alone. It is manifested as well in the interest displayed throughout the *1001 Nights* in the metaphoric value of words, the ability of a word to transfer its name and meaning to an object other than the one with which it is commonly affiliated, and to engender thereby a new meaning, a new object, and, correspondingly, a new reality. Metaphoric phrases and descriptions run rampant throughout the *1001 Nights* and freely embroider both descriptive and poetic pauses in the narrative. But nowhere is the significance of the metaphoric act as sharply underscored as it is in the suggestively ludic interlude in the frame story of "The Porter and the Three Ladies." In this cycle, which in its reliance on embedding techniques and in its initial determination by dominant female voices imitates the structure of the *1001 Nights* as a whole, are scattered clues that suggest answers to the questions about Shahrazad's apparent difference.

The interlude occurs shortly after the porter of the title, having charmed the women whom he has just encountered with his seeming verbal facility and intelligence, is granted leave to spend the evening in their company. Significantly, just before the interlude begins, the porter recites the following lines in response to an invitation to drain the wine cup:[3]

> I gave her pure old wine, red as her cheeks,
> Which with red fire did like a furnace glow.
> She kissed the brim and with a smile she asked,
> "How can you cheeks with cheeks pay what you owe?"
> I said, "Drink! This wine is my blood and tears,
> And my soul is the fragrance in the cup."
> She said, "If for me you have shed your blood,
> Most gladly will I on this red wine sup." (72)[4]

What is most significant about this poem is the conscious metaphorization that occurs within it and the gender opposition that accompanies it. The first hemistich hinges on the comparative particle *shibh*, "like," which is itself related to the word for simile, *tashbīh*. And indeed, the line initially presents as a simile the image from which the subsequent verses derive: the wine is *like* two red cheeks. In the following line, however, the simile is literalized in the woman's response to the offer. The comparative particle is suppressed and the comparison of the first line is interpreted—at this point ironically—as an established fact; it is, in fact, metaphorized. The wine then actually becomes the two red cheeks, but the laughing young woman who is the recipient of the process of metaphorization recognizes the problematic consequence of this act. If one posits a realm in which metaphors are affirmed, what becomes of the realm in which the metaphor has intervened? How do the literal and the metaphoric intersect and to which does one ultimately assign primacy? The third line of the poem resolves the issue. The central metaphor is explained through its further extensions, and the validity of metaphoric truth is thereby confirmed—a truth to which the young woman readily assents. The primacy of metaphor, as well as the poem as metaphor, is established.

The poem, then, tells about the process through which it, indeed all metaphor, is created. But at the same time, it also suggests a potential for gender opposition between the realm of the metaphoric and that of the literal which will be manipulated in the text to come. It is in this context that the following interlude is to be interpreted.

II

They carried on until they got drunk and the wine turned their heads. When the wine got the better of them, the doorkeeper went to the pool, took off her clothes, and stood stark naked, save for what was covered of her body by her loosened hair. Then she said, "Whee," went into the pool, and immersed herself in the water . . . and, after immersing herself completely, began to sport, taking water in her mouth and squirting it all over her sisters and the porter. Then she washed herself under her breasts, between her thighs, and inside her navel. Then she rushed out of the pool, sat naked in the porter's lap and, pointing to her slit, asked, "My lord and my love, what is this?" "Your womb," said he, and she replied, "Pooh, pooh, you have no shame," and slapped him on the neck. "Your vulva," said he, and the other sister pinched him, shouting, "Bah, this is an ugly word." "Your cunt," said he, and the third sister boxed him on the chest and knocked him over, saying, "Fie, have some shame." "Your clitoris," said he, and again the naked girl slapped him, saying, "No." "Your pudenda, your pussy, your sex tool," said he, and she kept replying, "No, no." He kept giving various other names, but every time he uttered a name, one of the girls hit him and asked, "What do you call this?" And they went on, this one boxing him, that one slapping him, another hitting him. At last, he turned to them and asked, "All right, what is its name?" The naked girl replied, "The basil of the bridges." The porter cried, "The basil of the bridges! You should have told me this from the beginning, oh, oh!" Then they passed the cup around and went on drinking for a while.

Then the shopper, like her sister, took off all her clothes, saying, "Whee," went into the pool, and immersed herself completely in the water. Then she washed herself under the belly, around the breasts, and between the thighs. Then she rushed out, threw herself in the porter's lap, and asked, "My little lord, what is this?" "Your vulva," said he, and she gave him a blow with which the hall resounded, saying, "Fie, you have no shame." "Your womb," said he, and her sister hit him, saying, "Fie, what an ugly word!" "Your clitoris," said he, and the other sister boxed him, saying, "Fie, fie, you are shameless." They kept at it, this one boxing him, that one slapping him, another hitting

17

him, another jabbing him, repeating, "No, no," while he kept shouting, "Your womb, your cunt, your pussy." Finally he cried, "The basil of the bridges," and all three burst out laughing till they fell on their backs. But again all three slapped him on the neck and said, "No, this is not its name." He cried, "All right, what is its name?" One of them replied, "Why don't you say 'the husked sesame'?" He cried out, "The husked sesame! Thank God we are finally there." Then the girl put on her clothes and they sat, passing the cup around, while the porter moaned with sore neck and shoulders.

They drank for a while, and then the eldest and fairest of the three stood up and began to undress. The porter touched his neck and began to rub it with his hand, saying, "For God's sake, spare my neck and shoulders," while the girl stripped naked, threw herself into the pool, and immersed herself. The porter looked at her naked body, which looked like a slice of the moon, and at her face, which shone like the full moon or the rising sun, and admired her figure, her breasts, and her swaying heavy hips, for she was naked as God had created her. Moaning, "Oh, oh," he addressed her with the following verses:

> If I compare your figure to the bough,
> When green, I err and a sore burden bear.
> The bough is fairest when covered with leaves,
> And you are fairest when completely bare.

When the girl heard his verses, she came quickly out of the pool, sat in his lap and, pointing to her slit, asked, "O light of my eyes, O sweetheart, what is the name of this?" "The basil of the bridges," said he, but she replied, "Bah!" "The husked sesame," said he, and she replied, "Pooh!" "Your womb," said he, and she replied, "Fie, you have no shame," and slapped him on the neck. To make a long story short, O King, the porter kept declaring, "Its name is so," and she kept saying "No, no, no, no." When he had had his fill of blows, pinches, and bites until his neck swelled and he choked and felt miserable, he cried out, "All right, what is its name?" She replied, "Why don't you

say the Inn of Abu Masrur?" "Ha, ha, the Inn of Abu
Masrur," said the porter. Then she got up, and after she
put on her clothes, they resumed their drinking and
passed the cup around for a while. (72–74)[5]

"The tale-teller's evident object is to accentuate the contrast with the tragical stories to follow," remarks Burton in a
footnote to the story, reading the passage in the light of the
bawdiness for which the *1001 Nights* is perhaps unjustly famous.[6] And yet the interlude, interpreted in the light of the
foregoing poem, suggests something far more telling.

At its most fundamental level, this frame-story passage can
be read as an inquiry into the way language functions within
the specific textual realm of the three ladies: a questioning of
the relation between a thing and the word by which it is
named, as well as of the way in which that name is communicated. "What is the name of this?" demands each of the
women in turn, and the simple porter, having apparently
forgotten the lesson implied in his metaphoric poem, can
only reply with the most literal, indeed, the most clinical,
and, to the women, the most offensive of terms. Three times,
he offers the doorkeeper the words that identify the indicated object in the realm of the everyday here and now, and
three times he is punished for his reply. When he tries with
the second woman to profit from the phraseology learned
from his first experience, he is no more successful; and by
the time he is tried by the third woman, he seems to have lost
all real initiative: "To make a long story short, O King, the
porter kept declaring, 'Its name is so,'" reports Shahrazad,
no longer bothering to quote the porter directly.

The problem clearly is that the porter is unable to make
either the conceptual or the linguistic leap from the literal to
the figurative realm, to cross over from what classical Arabic
rhetoricians term *al-lughah al-ḥaqīqīyah*, real, literal language,
to *al-lughah al-majāzīyah*, figurative, tropic language. He fails

to realize what the great Arab theorist of metaphor ʿAbd al-Qāhir al-Jurjānī codified in his work on rhetoric, *Dalāʾil al-Iʿjāz:* that language is of two kinds. Kamal Abu Deeb, al-Jurjānī's translator and interpreter, explains the division in the following way:

> In the first type, the general purport (*gharaḍ*) is conveyed by the *significance* of the expression itself, such as when one says, "Zaid went out," to assert in an immediate way the going out of Zaid. . . . In the second type, it is not possible to realize the intention through the immediate significance of the expression alone: first the expression conveys its meaning which is presupposed by the linguistic usage, then one finds that this meaning has a second significance, the understanding of which leads to the realization of the intention. This type is the one where a usage of *kināya, istiʿāra,* or *tamthīl* occurs.[7]

Clearly, at this point in the tale the porter inhabits a linguistic universe that functions according to the rules determined by the first kind of language, a realm where words mean exactly what they say, where communication is effected immediately by the words expressed. He has, temporarily at least, lapsed into a world of unambiguous meaning and clearly defined linguistic borders. In short, his affiliation with the prosaic has been asserted.

The three ladies, needless to say, do not share this affiliation. Indeed, from the outset of the tale they have been portrayed as moving within a world decidedly separate from that of the porter, a world whose outer spatial limit is determined by the imposing double door inlaid with ivory and gold. Once this threshold is crossed, one enters a feminine realm where reality loses its literal cast and no longer accords with al-Jurjānī's first category of language. Significant in this respect are the various descriptions given of the women. All three are focalized through the porter, but only the first is registered before he reaches the threshold. Thus we are told of the provisioness at the opening of the tale that she wore

> a Mosul cloak, a silk veil, a fine kerchief embroidered with
> gold, and a pair of leggings tied with fluttering laces.
> When she lifted her veil, she revealed a pair of beautiful
> dark eyes graced with long lashes and a tender expression,
> like those celebrated by the poets. (66–67)[8]

The description is direct and for all intents and purposes
nonfigurative, the general meaning being conveyed, in al-
Jurjānī's terms, by the significance of the expression. The
woman's clothing is accurately described, as are her all-
important eyes and glance. And even though the narrator
refers to the descriptions of other poets, the poems themselves are not quoted. In short, the correspondence between
word and thing in this description is as unambiguous as
possible. We are still within the realm of the literal.

The second woman occupies a liminal position, for it is
she who beckons to the porter from beyond the threshold,
inviting him to cross the borderline. "Sister, what are you
waiting for? Come in and relieve this poor man of his heavy
burden" (69).[9] Hers is the longest, most detailed description.

> The porter, looking to see who opened the door, saw a
> full-bosomed girl, about five feet tall. She was all charm,
> beauty, and perfect grace, with a forehead like the new
> moon, eyes like those of a deer or wild heifer, eyebrows
> like the crescent in the month of Sha'ban, cheeks like red
> anemones, mouth like the seal of Solomon, lips like red
> carnelian, teeth like a row of pearls set in coral, neck like a
> cake for a king, bosom like a fountain, breasts like a pair of
> big pomegranates resembling a rabbit with uplifted ears,
> and belly with a navel like a cup that holds a pound of
> benzoin ointment. She was like her of whom the poet aptly
> said:
>
> > On stately sun and full moon cast your sight;
> > Savor the flowers and lavender's delight.
> > Your eyes have never seen such white in black,

Such radiant face with hair so deeply dark.
With rosy cheeks, Beauty proclaimed her name,
To those who had not yet received her fame.
Her swaying heavy hips I joyed to see,
But her sweet, slender waist brought tears to me.
    (68–69)[10]

The difference between the two passages is immediately obvious. Whereas the first description is couched in the language of direct reference, the second is mediated through the trope of simile. The opening literal statement of the description—"The porter, looking to see who opened the door, saw a full-bosomed girl, about five feet tall"—gives way immediately to figurative language. The language of this passage does not function directly; the link between word and object is here not the only, not even the primary one, for the meaning is deflected through the comparative particle "like," *ka*. The doorkeeper's eyebrows are not simply eyebrows; they are *like* the crescent moon at Sha'ban; her teeth are not just white; they are like a row of pearls set in coral. The primacy of the reference of ordinary language is tempered by the possibility of a second reference suggested in the comparative component of the simile. Ordinary reference is not canceled, but it is supplemented by a further nonliteral reference. The line between the literal and the tropic is straddled, for the simile, while literally accurate, suggests the possibility of metaphoric expression.[11] The poem, which this time is cited, functions as a similar link between the literal and the figurative realms. Although it opens with an exhortation that might be metaphorically construed (the woman is like the stately sun and full moon on which we are to gaze), the description quickly limits itself largely to a kind of straightforward, descriptive language, noting unambiguously such attributes as the woman's deeply dark hair and sweet, slender waist. We are standing with the porter on the threshold of the figurative.

The third woman, significantly, stands at an even further

spatial remove from the observer. Found inside a black juniper-wood couch inlaid with gems and pearls and hung with red silk curtains, she is a woman

> with genial charm, wise mien, and features as radiant as the moon. She had an elegant figure, the scent of ambergris, sugared lips, Babylonian eyes, with eyebrows as arched as a pair of bent bows, and a face whose radiance put the shining sun to shame, for she was like a great star soaring in the heavens, or a dome of gold, or an unveiled bride, or a splendid fish swimming in a fountain, or a morsel of luscious fat in a bowl of milk soup. She was like her of whom the poet said:
>
> > Her smile reveals twin rows of pearls
> > Or white daisies or pearly hail.
> > Her forelock like the night unfurls;
> > Before her light the sun is pale. (69)[12]

This is the only one of the three descriptions in which metaphoric language has taken hold. Although the description again opens with a direct literal statement (the woman has genial charm and a wise mien) and closes with an elaborate string of similes (she was like a great star soaring in the heavens, or a dome of gold, or an unveiled bride, etc.), the intervening segment is cast in clearly metaphorical language. The woman's features are lunar (Haddawy's more elegant translation turns the metaphor into a simile: "features radiant as the moon"); her lips are sugared. And similarly, her face that shames the shining sun and her alif-like stature (this is the literal translation of Haddawy's "elegant figure," a phrase that works against the metaphoric value of the original), no matter how accessible as metaphors, must be interpreted figuratively if they are to make sense within the accepted semantic confines of the language. The phrase "alif-like stature," for example, has no literal meaning, at least no logical literal meaning within the realm of ordinary linguistic usage when applied to a woman. The literal reference of the word *alif* must be suspended, then, and a second-order reference,[13] a reference secondary to the primary one, be supplied in order to complete the meaning. Thus the reader calls up the pertinent notions of slenderness and straightness suggested in the embodiment of the letter signified by the word *alif* and subsequently makes the comparisons and substitutions necessary for significant meaning.

The poem that concludes the description sustains the necessity of this kind of metaphoric reading. This time, no literal descriptive statements aid in our imaging what this beautiful woman looks like. The poem operates strictly on the figurative level. The woman's teeth are pearls or daisies or hail; her forelock is like the night. In order to understand the meaning of the passage fully, we must understand the process of metaphoric transference or borrowing, *isti'ārah*. al-Jurjānī, again in *Dalā'il al-I'jāz*, describes the process in the following way:

> We know that you do not say: "I saw a lion" [when describing a man] unless you have the purpose of attributing to the man the same status of the lion, in his courage, daring, the power of his attack, and his unhesitant nature as well as attributing to him the quality of never feeling fear and never being in a state of terror. One also knows that if the hearer understands this meaning, he does not understand it from the word "lion" itself but by understanding its meaning.[14]

One moves from an acknowledgment of the literal reference of the term, what al-Jurjānī calls in another passage "the meaning," *al-ma'nā*, to a recognition of the implications, the secondary characteristics of the term, "the meaning of the meaning," *ma'nā al-ma'nā*.[15] In this movement lies the power of metaphor.

Curiously, the only poem that intervenes in the interlude discussed earlier seemingly undercuts this metaphoric movement by warning against the dangers of false analogy (*qiyās*, from the verb *qāsa*, "to compare," which opens the poem) and, by implication, of weak metaphors. False comparisons, the poem suggests, conceal reality, distort the fundamental truth of an object; whereas referring to the object as in itself it truly is, bared of all figurative language, reveals its true essence. ("If I compare your figure to the bough, / When green, I err and a sore burden bear. / The bough is fairest when covered with leaves, / And you are fairest when completely bare.") And yet the porter himself, despite his poetic caution, has no choice if he is to continue in the company of these women but to learn to operate in the metaphoric realm. He is, for the moment, ineluctably caught within the feminine realm and the grasp of metaphor.

III

It is in this light, then, that the interlude between the porter and the three ladies is to be read. When each of the women in turn demands the name of that part of her body which should, in polite society, remain unnameable, she is, clearly, demanding the metaphoric name, the name that, in one sense, covers up the literality of the exposed object. To some extent, the language of the passage underscores this suggestion. When, for example, the porter is unable to respond appropriately to the question asked by all three of the ladies—either what is this or what is its name—he is tellingly struck repeatedly on the back of his neck. The verb used most often to describe this action is *ḍaraba,* meaning "to hit" or "to strike," but also having the associate meaning "to coin." Hence the expression *ḍarb mathal li-shay',* the coining of a likeness for something, to define the rhetorical term *tamthīl,* "likeness" or "comparison."[16] The possibility of indirect, figurative expression, couched in the means of punishment for refusing to respond to this very possibility, is strongly implied at least four times. But the porter is, not surprisingly, unable to comprehend anything beyond the immediate physical significance of the language and its corresponding action.

It should be noted here that there is in traditional Arabic rhetoric a tropic device, *kināyah,* by means of which a word that, because of either social, cultural, or linguistic conventions, should not be expressed is replaced by a word or words that must be interpreted figuratively. The euphemistic value of this device is of particular importance. As Charles Pellat notes in an article on *kināyah:* "It is a case of euphemisms whose purpose is to 'palliate the ugly' (*taḥsīn al-qabīḥ*), as al-Thaʿālibī says, and it is the examples of this genre that the authors most often quote . . . ; generally they concern woman, the sexual organs, defecation, various forms of uncleanness and everything which is of bad omen."[17]

There is obviously a connection between this kind of euphemism and the word games of the three women. One could consider at length the inclusion of women in the cataloging of things whose ugliness needs to be palliated, but for the moment there are two other things that should be remarked upon: First, the term *kināyah* is usually translated in English as metonymy; and although it is generally listed as a subcategory of metaphor, it necessitates, by definition, a logical, contiguous relation between the term and its replacement—a connection that metaphor shuns and that is clearly not in evidence in the substitutions made by the ladies. Second, the self-consciousness of the text, the degree to which it foregrounds the replacement of one term by another, radically undercuts the euphemistic value that rightfully belongs to *kināyah,* as does the fact that it is the women themselves who are manipulating this trope as it relates to their own bodies. The women are not trying to conceal the proper term of their metaphor. They are, on the contrary, doing everything they can to make the connection with its metaphoric replacement obvious. Far from tempering any potential embarrassment or humiliation that might result from uncovering their bodies, the three women are instead proclaiming their difference.

What the women are ultimately doing is initiating the porter into a universe in which theirs is the dominant voice, in which the metaphoric holds sway. Metaphor, remarks Aristotle in the *Rhetoric,* is a kind of enigma. It consists, he notes in the *Poetics,* in giving the thing a name that belongs to something else.[18] What is the name of this, ask the women; to which the porter, having exhausted the literal possibilities, can only reply: What is its name then? Identification within the literal realm leads to naming within the figurative realm, and metaphor ensues. It is this very type of metaphoric transaction that Christine Brooke-Rose identifies in *The Grammar of Metaphor* as a pointing formula: the proper term A is replaced by the metaphor B with some demonstrative expression pointing back to the proper term.[19] Thus the three ladies point to the object to be named, replace it with the demonstrative pronoun *this,* and finally offer the metaphoric replacement. In so doing, they show the porter how metaphor is made, foreground the process in which the literal name of a thing is replaced by a figurative expression.

The porter, it would seem, is not the most apt pupil, despite his earlier successful foray into the metaphoric universe. Three times the women repeat the same enigmatic question, and three times the porter fails in his response. "Have some shame," scolds the first lady in a sentiment echoed by the second, in an effort, perhaps, to shame the porter into crossing the border between the literal realm he inhabits and the metaphoric realm of the three ladies. But the porter clings tenaciously to those words which for him best nominate the things in the universe he has, until recently, inhabited. Until all of a sudden, for no apparent reason except that the lesson is over and he has had time to reflect, he linguistically ventures forth:

> Then the porter stood up, took off his clothes, and, revealing something dangling between his legs, he leapt and plunged into the middle of the pool . . . then he rushed out of the pool, planted himself in the lap of the fairest girl, put his arms on the lap of the doorkeeper, rested his

legs in the lap of the shopper and, pointing to his penis, asked, "Ladies, what is this?" They were pleased with his antics and laughed, for his disposition agreed with theirs, and they found him entertaining. One of them said, "Your cock," and he replied, "You have no shame; this is an ugly word." The other said, "Your penis," and he replied, "You should be ashamed; may God put you to shame." The third said, "Your dick," and he replied, "No." Another said, "Your stick," and he replied, "No." Another said, "Your thing, your testicles, your prick," and he kept saying, "No, no, no." They asked, "What is the name of this?" He hugged this and kissed that, pinched the one, bit the other, and nibbled on the third, as he took satisfaction, while they laughed until they fell on their backs. At last they asked, "Friend, what is its name?" The porter replied, "Don't you know its name? It is the smashing mule." They asked, "What is the meaning of the name the smashing mule?" He replied, "It is the one who grazes in the basil of the bridges, eats the husked sesame, and gallops in the Inn of Abu Masrur." Again they laughed until they fell on their backs and almost fainted with laughter. (74–75)[20]

The porter appears to have learned his lesson well after all, for the passage repeats exactly the format established previously by the three women. There are, nonetheless, two fundamental differences. The first is found in the way in which the women respond to the porter's questioning. The mirthfulness with which they accompany their literal replies underscores the ludic, almost ornamental aspect of the exchange, and it is enforced by the affectionate behavior with which the porter counters them. But more important is the final reply of the porter himself. For although he shows himself capable of metaphoric expression, he also displays his utter reliance on the women's tutelage. The porter has indeed created a complete and completely metaphoric sentence, but except for its initial element, it depends entirely on the phrases specified by the women. And further, the subject term itself, the "smashing mule," suggests a kind of deep, abiding unwillingness, indeed inability, to understand

and to change accordingly. The porter is still not able to function independently within the metaphoric universe.

IV

He has, however, for the time being at least, accepted the women's invitation to join them in their universe, agreed to sunder his ties with the world at large, the world of ordinary, literal reference, and affiliate himself with the transformational realm of metaphor. In order to do so, he has had to learn the various codes that determine any society, real, fictive, or figurative. But most important, he has had to learn the language, crack the code by which verbal communication is effected in the feminine realm. Thus the symbolic value of the porter's final reply, for even if he has not demonstrated a strongly original metaphoric talent, he has indicated that he understands, at last, the language spoken by the three ladies. He has become a partner in their linguistic community.

All ordinary discourse implies this kind of partnership, of course. Linguists at least since Saussure have asserted that in order for language to communicate, there has to be an agreement—usually tacit—among the participants of the speech act as to what the individual semantic components mean. But so implicit is this agreement in any everyday linguistic transaction that, except in cases of obvious misunderstanding which require clarification of the intended meaning, it is never questioned, never heightened, never foregrounded. Communication, then, can occur without drawing undue attention to the partnership implied.

Such is not the case with the communication and subsequent interpretation of figurative and, especially, metaphoric language. As Ted Cohen remarks in an article entitled "Metaphor and the Cultivation of Intimacy":

> There is a unique way in which the maker and the appreciator of a metaphor are drawn closer to one another. Three aspects are involved: (1) the speaker issues a kind of

concealed invitation; (2) the hearer expends a special effort to accept the invitation; and (3) this transaction constitutes the acknowledgment of a community. All three are
involved in any communication, but in ordinary literal discourse their involvement is so pervasive and routine that
they go unremarked. The use of metaphor throws them
into relief, and there is a point in that.[21]

Metaphor does not mean the way ordinary language does,
does not communicate directly, unambiguously, the way literal discourse does. If, in simplistic terms, we accept ordinary language as the direct conveyer of an intended meaning, we in consequence accept such language as "true," as
meaning what it says. Metaphoric language allows for no
such acceptance, for most metaphorical statements are pat-
ently false. If they are to communicate effectively, they require conscious acknowledgment that the expression has
been received as a metaphor, decoded, and subsequently
interpreted. When the first lady points to her genitals and
tells the porter that their name is the basil of the bridges, the
porter (and, of course, the woman and the reader as well)
knows that the statement is false. The woman has issued an
invitation to the porter to join her in the metaphoric realm;
but the porter does not, indeed cannot, accept the invitation
until he has learned the rules of the game, at which point he
accepts the invitation by replying in the women's own terms.

The result of such a transaction, according to Cohen, is
the achievement of a certain intimacy between the communi-
cants, an intimacy instigated by the issuing and accepting of
the metaphoric invitation. Cohen explains it in the following
manner: "He [the listener] must penetrate your remark, so
to speak, in order to explore you yourself, in order to grasp
the import. . . . Furthermore, you know that he is doing this;
you have invited him to do it; you have, in fact, required him
to do it. He accepts the requirement, and you two become an
intimate pair."[22] But such intimacy is furthered in the act of
interpretation itself; for if, as remarked above, literal lan-

guage is generally accessible to all who know its linguistic code, the comprehension of figurative language is restricted to those who share a certain knowledge about one another, have a kind of complicit understanding of one another's values, beliefs, and intentions. The porter, clearly, is at a disadvantage in this respect, for although the women find that his disposition agrees with theirs, his acquaintance with the women is short-lived and his gender, values, and frame of reference essentially different from their own. But in the act of uncovering themselves in his presence, the three ladies literally and metaphorically reveal themselves to the porter and in so doing share with him that information he needs to decipher their metaphors. A fundamental intimacy is thereby achieved.

V

The intimacy achieved between the porter and the three ladies goes beyond the sharing of a certain knowledge. For if the ladies reveal themselves to the porter in order to help him to decode their metaphors, the very nature of their action also invites him to enjoy a further and perhaps corollary intimacy with them. That intimacy is, of course, never completely achieved; the porter's relations with the women never move beyond the suggestive, flirtatious stage. Indeed, he is, we are told in the very first line of the story, a bachelor, and in a curious interpolation Burton adds that he would remain that way until the end of his days. Nonetheless, the implications of this possible sexual intimacy are interesting and far-ranging for a reading of the *1001 Nights* as a whole.

The metaphoric disguise in which the women dress their physical references is not an uncommon device in the *Nights*. Rarely does one encounter a literal description of physical aspect, particularly if the beauty of the person in question seemingly surpasses all natural limits; but more rare still are literally explicit statements referring to sexual matters. The tropic figure of *kināyah* was mentioned above, and to a certain extent euphemistic concerns are at work in the figurative deflection of explicit sexual reference. But if one looks more closely at the metaphoric concealment of the body in all its aspects, one learns an interesting lesson about the nature of narrative in the *1001 Nights*.

"Il paraît," remarks Roland Barthes in *Le plaisir du texte,* "que les érudits arabes, en parlant du texte, emploient cette expression admirable: *le corps certain.*"[23] Barthes's source is unspecified, but the possible validity and implications of such a statement are clear. We are, after all, in a textual universe where women have the bearing of an alif, where the fullness of a stomach suggests the scroll of a book, and where language is taught by renaming the female body. If the body can, metaphorically speaking, be a text, then the text can, in return, be a body. The metaphoric qualification is essential, however.

There is a strong association between textual/narrative activity and sexual activity which lies at the heart of the *1001 Nights,* and which in some sense actually engenders the work. From the start, from before the first night has even begun, the supreme tale-teller makes the connection explicit. "Sister, listen well to what I am telling you," says Shahrazad. "When I go to the king, I will send for you, and when you come and see that the king has finished with me, say, 'Sister, if you are not sleepy, tell us a story.' Then I will begin to tell a story, and it will cause the king to stop his practice, save myself, and deliver the people" (16).[24]

The connection between the two nocturnal activities is clear. The humanly creative aspect of the sexual act is mirrored in the textually creative aspect of the verbal act. In this case, the one potentially generative activity leads to, in fact instigates, the other. One must not forget that Shahrazad has borne three children during the course of the 1001 nights and that these children are the bargaining chips she uses to convince Shahrayar to release her from captivity. They are, in a sense, the objective correlative or, perhaps more precisely, the metaphoric equivalent of her narrative activity.

The connection between the physical and the textual is not always so explicitly maintained. In a late tale not included in the Mahdi edition, for example, an adulterous act of physical union is described in the following way (the translation is Burton's): "Then he spent the rest of the night with her in embracing and clipping, plying the particle of copulation in concert and joining the conjunctive with the conjoined, whilst her husband was as a cast-out nunnation of construction."[25] The description of the sexual element here depends upon a metaphorization based not on overt references to narrative activity as such but rather on the grammatical structure necessary to the text. The lovers are physically conjoined in a fashion that is repeated in the grammatical act of conjunction, the joining of one linguistic unit to another; while the rejected husband, in a reference to a rule of Arabic grammar, is likened to the superfluous and therefore invalid particle of definition in *iḍāfah,* genitive construction.[26] Through their metaphorization, then, the individual elements of the proper term, the three elements implied in the adulterous couple, assume the status of the separate units that, when grammatically positioned, create a text, potentially engender narrative.

We return to our tale. The three ladies, it would seem, are fundamentally implicated in this connection between intercourse and discourse, between body and text. For if the one is a metaphor for the other, the women's lesson about metaphor and the way they choose to give this lesson are even more significant. In a discussion of the metaphorical process, Paul Ricoeur makes the following observation: "The very expression 'figure of speech' implies that in metaphor, as in the other tropes or turns, discourse assumes the nature of a body by displaying forms and traits which usually characterize the human face, man's 'figure'; it is as though the tropes give to discourse a quasi-bodily externalization."[27] Metaphor, then, shares in the corporal status of the text. Indeed, if the text metaphorically poses as a body, metaphor supplies the features and traits that compose that body. When the three ladies try to teach the porter about metaphor by tropically naming their sexual organs, they are also teaching him a lesson about the way metaphor, in their separate, well-defined universe, is related to narrative, about the way and kind of narrative metaphor generates and engenders.

VI

I have remarked above that the *1001 Nights* is a work that is premised upon a kind of fundamental gender opposition, and that allows its heroines to speak, at least for a time, in their own distinctive voices, thereby suggesting the potential for a realm in which women wield the real power within the text. (I will argue later that this potential is never truly realized.) Shahrazad is the quintessential heroine in this regard, and as such she gives her female characters, many of whom are themselves narrative-women, the lead. The three ladies of this tale—two of whom will have stories of their own to tell later in the cycle, though only once they are outside their privileged, feminine space—are clearly intent upon creating a narrative environment that will support, indeed highlight, their own storytelling activity. I noted earlier the definite spatial borders that divide the realm of the three ladies from that of the porter. What should be clear at this point is that there is a corresponding linguistic division that separates the porter from his female companions at this moment in the text and that is re-created in the women's demand further on in the frame tale that the men who have joined them for the evening either tell their tales in a fashion pleasing to them or be permanently silenced.

What is going on here is the establishment of a specific kind of discourse as defined by the three ladies of this tale, a discourse that focuses on the female body and on the relation of this body to metaphoric language. The sexually suggestive language the women try to teach the porter clearly has no place or, more accurately, no meaningful translation within the prosaic, masculine realm inhabited by their guest. Indeed, even metaphor in the world of the three ladies doesn't function according to the rules of the game in the outside linguistic realm, since for at least two of the three terms offered by the women—the basil of the bridges and husked sesame—there is no recognizable relationship of similarity between the metaphoric term and the female genitals. This is not the case with the third phrase. The Inn (or resting place) of Abu Masrur does indeed acknowledge a "real" correspondence between the literal term and its metaphoric replacement; but this relationship is, significantly, one necessarily dependent on an interrelationship between male and female, and one might well argue that this third and final phrase is the result of a generous gesture on the part of the three women to help the porter with his linguistic lesson.

On the whole, however, one is here not far from a kind of *écriture féminine*. What the three ladies are doing in this part of the story, which instigates the subsequent narrative activity of the cycle, is privileging a narrative universe in which the dictates of a particular kind of women's discourse provide the standards for linguistic and narrative interaction and play. In allowing the porter (and later the three dervishes, Harun al-Rashid and his two companions) to enter this realm, the three ladies not only indicate what the dominant social, sexual, and linguistic factors within their society are (as Shahrazad has done before them) but also kindly offer to teach their male companions the rules of their games—social, sexual, linguistic, and otherwise—a gesture that will, unhappily, ultimately prove fruitless. One suspects that in so doing, the women are trying to remedy the kind of serious and apparently inevitable division between the sexes that forms the narrative core of the subsequent stories, both their own and those of their guests—all stories of either political, social, or, especially, romantic division and disruption. It is indeed significant in this light that the closing frame of the cycle ends, not unlike many a nineteenth-century novel, with the pairing of all those narrative-men and -women we have encountered in the cycle's course.

Except, of course, that the universe in which this happy ending has been effected has been influenced not in the least by the dictates of "realism," as have so many of those nineteenth-century textual universes. I would argue that this is due in part to the suggested relation between metaphor and narrative in "The Porter and the Three Ladies." If, as Aristotle remarks, metaphor consists in giving the thing a name that belongs to something else, metaphor becomes an instrument to break the referentiality of language, to deliver language from its ontological function. Metaphor allows language to transcend its "real" limits. In so doing, it refashions the reality to which this language refers, gestures toward a realm in which the metaphoric term has meaning, a realm that by definition cannot correspond to the one referred to by ordinary, literal, nonfigurative language. Metaphor thus imbues language with a powerful aspect that lets us forget the already established world, and carries us over into a realm in which words speak of things that are not accessible to ordinary human view.

The realm into which metaphor so readily carries us is the textual one, where the transformational power of the word can be fully effected. Metaphor generates the narrative sphere, in which words need not correspond to a predetermined reality, in which words have the power to create their own reality. Herein lies the fundamental lesson of our tale's interlude. For we must not forget that the main interaction between the porter and the three ladies occurs in the frame story, in that part of the story which instigates the subsequent narrative activity. Indeed, the cycle is, like that of Sindbad or the Hunchback, generated uniquely by the act of storytelling, an aspect in which it imitates the *1001 Nights* as a whole. In schooling the porter in metaphor, the ladies are not only initiating him into the secrets of their sex but teaching him about the way in which metaphor can create a specific kind of narrative, about the way in which the breaking of the referentiality of language can give access to a new and much-desired realm.

The porter, however, is excluded from this happy ending, for ultimately he has no story to tell. When confronted with the necessity of making narrative amends for his transgression, he can only reply: "Mistress, you know that the reason I came to this place was that I was hired as a porter by this shopper, who led me from the vintner to the butcher, and from the butcher to the greengrocer, and from the greengrocer to the fruit vendor, and from the fruit vendor to the drygrocer, then to the confectioner, to the druggist, and finally to this house. This is my tale" (86).[28]

The porter sticks so scrupulously to the literal facts of his story that there is nothing to report except the basic itinerary that gets him from one place to another. The very vocabulary of this brief synopsis—the juxtaposition of *ḥammāl*, "porter," and *ḥammalatnī*, "she hired me as a porter"—and the final, elliptical phrase, "this is my tale," indicate the porter's meager verbal resources. The narrative, if such it can be called, is the final proof that the porter will never be able to make the linguistic leap necessary to cross over into the universe inhabited by the women. Not only will he remain unmarried, but he will remain within the linguistic and geographical confines of the real world of medieval Baghdad, never to cross the frontiers that would allow him to move beyond the stage of narrative and sexual flirtation. Once his simple story is told, the porter fades into the narrative background of his cycle and assumes the unobtrusive position of audience. His final words are a demand that he be allowed to hear the stories of his companions. We never hear from him again.

Chapter Three

Realigning the Narrative Lines
Metonymic and Metaphoric Affiliations

Let us suppose that archaeologists of the future coming from another planet would one day, when all human life had disappeared from the earth, excavate one of our libraries. . . . However they would soon find out that a whole category of books did not fit the usual pattern: these would be the orchestra scores on the shelves of the music division. But after trying, without success, to decipher staffs one after the other, from the upper down to the lower, they would probably notice that the same patterns of notes recurred at intervals, either in full or in part, or that some patterns were strongly reminiscent of earlier ones. Hence the hypothesis: what if patterns showing affinity, instead of being considered in succession, were to be treated as one complex pattern and read globally? By getting at what we call *harmony*, they would then find out that an orchestra score, in order to become meaningful, has to be read diachronically along one axis—that is, page after page, and from left to right—and also synchronically along the other axis, all the notes which are written vertically making up one gross constituent unit, i.e., one bundle of relations.

—Claude Lévi-Strauss, *The Structural Study of Myth*

I

THE narrative act in the *1001 Nights* is the most important act that can be performed within this textual universe. Any narrative, no matter how primitive, has the potential to prolong life, to forestall death, just as the absence of narrative (witness the wordless and poisoned page of Sage Duban's book) promises certain death.[1] Shahrazad provides the sterling example of the narrator who succeeds in staving off and ultimately avoiding death by telling stories, and in so doing she functions as a kind of role model for the subsequent narrators of her tales. The three ladies cycle offers a case in point. Indeed, the use of the frame-story structure in this cycle (as in others) insists upon the parallel with the larger frame story of the *1001 Nights* as a whole. The porter's feeble narrative effort is, after all, prefaced by the command of the eldest Baghdadian woman: "Whoever tells us his tale and explains what has happened to him and what has brought him to our place, let him stroke his head and go, but whoever refuses, strike off his head" (85).[2]

Once the precedent is established, the three dervishes need no further encouragement. As their individual tales indicate, they are well acquainted with the power of narrative and have learned the art of storytelling well. The doorkeeper and the eldest lady, in turn, follow suit upon royal command. (The provisioness, who through her mercantile activities has affiliated herself with the everyday realm of the here and now, has, like the porter, no story to tell.) Once each has said his or her narrative piece, the frame is closed and the cycle brought to an end.

The actual manipulation of the narrative act is, of course, far more complicated than that just sketched. Once beyond the frame story, the narrative act continues to be repeated within the individual tales. So pronounced is this phenomenon that in his essay on the *1001 Nights,* Tzvetan Todorov generalizes it into a law of narrative development: "Le personnage, c'est une histoire virtuelle qui est l'histoire de sa vie. Tout nouveau personnage signifie une nouvelle intrigue. Nous sommes dans le royaume des hommes-récits."[3] It is not as characters, as fully developed personnages with distinctive traits and characteristics, that we know the principal characters of our cycle but rather as narrative functionaries whose primary indeed sole responsibility is to further the development of the narrative context.

Todorov links the role of these narrative-men to the formal device of embedding, that narrative structure by which one tale contains another tale that in turn contains a third. It is this device that best represents the significance of the narrative act in the *1001 Nights.* As Todorov remarks: "L'enchâssement est une mise en évidence d'une propriété essentielle de tout récit. Car le récit enchâssant, c'est *le récit d'un récit.* En racontant l'histoire d'un autre récit, le premier atteint son thème secret et en même temps se réfléchit dans cette image de soi-même."[4] The essential function of this kind of narrative is to talk about itself, to reflect back upon itself, and in so doing to reproduce itself. Embedded structures, in both their active and passive forms, provide the forum within which this self-reflective activity can most effectively take place. Not surprisingly, it is to the frame story, that narrative segment which is the primary generator of embedded stories, that one must look for the most significant account of the narrative function.

Within the frame story of "The Porter and the Three Ladies," the power of narrative, or, more specifically, the power of the verbal act, has already taken hold. The porter, remember, initially convinces the three ladies to let him share in their company by displaying his intelligence and corresponding verbal virtuosity:

> Trust me; I am a sensible and wise man. I have studied the sciences and attained knowledge; I have read and learned, and presented my knowledge and cited my authorities. I reveal the good and conceal the bad, and I am well-behaved. I am like the man of whom the poet said:
>
>> Only the faithful does a secret keep;
>> None but the best can hold it unrevealed.
>> I keep a secret in a well-shut house
>> Of which the key is lost and the lock sealed. (71)[5]

The ladies are suitably impressed by the porter's linguistic skill and narrative promise and accept them as a substitute for the monetary remuneration they would ordinarily receive for their hospitality. Similarly, when the three dervishes arrive, the porter, in his turn, requests a similar kind of payment: "Then the porter asked, 'Friends, can you entertain us with something?'" (77).[6]

The dervishes know better than to squander their narrative gifts at such an offhand request and present instead a musical offering that in its harmonious aspect promises their narrative skills to come. It is not, in fact, until Harun al-Rashid and his attendants appear at the magic door that a full-fledged narrative is offered, first in the voice of Shahrazad:

> Now the cause of that knocking, O King, was that it happened on that very night that the Caliph Harun al-Rashid and Ja'far came into the city, as they used to do every now and then, and as they walked through, they passed by the door and heard the music of the flute, the harp, and the tambourine, the singing of the girls, and the sounds of people partying and laughing. (77–78)[7]

The story is then continued in the first-person voice of Ja'far himself: "O my lady, we are merchants from the city of Mosul, and we have been in Baghdad for ten days" (78).[8]

The inevitable corollary to this simultaneous desire for narrative on the part of the audience and impulse toward narrative on the part of the speaker is an overriding injunction against narrative curiosity imposed by the legislators of this narrative realm. It is upon the porter that this condition is placed initially and consequently most forcefully. Not only do the three ladies warn the porter of the dangers of verbal indiscretion, but they fortify their spoken warning by making him recite its written complement, which is, significantly, engraved over the liminally positioned door:

> They said, "You cannot spend the night with us unless you agree to abide by our condition, that whatever we do and whatever happens to us, you shall refrain from asking for any explanation, for 'speak not of what concerns you not, lest you hear what pleases you not.' This is our condition; don't be too curious about any action of ours." He replied, "Yes, yes, yes, I am dumb and blind." They said, "Rise, then, go to the entrance, and read what is inscribed on the door and the entrance." He got up, went to the door and found on the door and the entrance the following inscription written in letters of gold, "Whoever speaks of what concerns him not hears what pleases him not." The porter came back and said, "I pledge to you that I will not speak of what concerns me not." (76)[9]

The condition is not placed upon the porter alone. When the three dervishes appear, they are granted shelter only if they agree to the same condition, a restriction of which they are rather imperiously reminded by the porter. And when the third set of visitors arrives, the condition is once again repeated in full.

Ultimately, however, a conflict of authorities, a struggle between one legislative body and another, ensues, for the caliph, accustomed to wielding absolute power within his realm, is unable to submit to the jurisdiction of the three ladies within their own. It is he who, when confronted with the cryptic behavior of the three women, instigates, against

Ja'far's counsel, the rebellious questioning of the porter and thereby intentionally violates the repeated injunction. And although he manages to escape his deserved punishment through the verbal offices of Ja'far, he is still unwilling to forgo his royal prerogative of audience. Once back within his own domain, he further satisfies his narrative curiosity by ordering the three women to make their own narrative amends.

In this he is following their lead, for the three women themselves have already been caught in the narrative web. They have, as noted above, succumbed to the porter's initial request because of his apparent verbal gift, and as further proof of this acceptance, they have revealed to him the linguistic code of their domain. When the porter, as spokesman for the group, requests clarification of their mysterious actions, the ladies feel that their social and corresponding linguistic code has been broken. The punishment for such infraction is, as always, death; but true to the larger laws governing this textual universe, such sure death can be deflected by the power of narrative. It takes no more than the porter's meager poetic response to break the ladies' anger;[10] no more than the dervishes' promise of intriguing narratives to remind the women of what they surely once knew: that a good story is an acceptable ransom for a man's life.

No one, then, escapes from the desire for narrative in the frame story. If the porter, dervishes, and caliph are willing to risk their lives in the quest for narrative, the women, in their turn, are willing to spare them in the same interest. There is something obsessive, if not, strictly speaking, pathological, in this desire for narrative, a desire that suggests that any act—no matter how transgressive—can be compensated for by its narrative equivalent; that any act is worth committing in order to have the pleasure of recounting its narrative equivalent. Desire for narrative, desire in narrative, desire and narrative: they are the two basic elements that combine and recombine to structure both the frame story and the narratives it engenders.

II

We return, inevitably, to the interlude. I earlier made the connection between the metaphoric games played by the porter and the women and the physical intimacy achieved in the playing of these games. Again, this connection lies at the heart of the *1001 Nights:* sexual activity engenders and ultimately equals narrative activity; Shahrazad's nights with the king satisfy not only his sexual desire but his narrative desire as well. The interlude makes the relationship even more explicit, for the underpinnings of this textual universe, the workings of metaphor, are revealed in the guise of sexual play. It is no accident that desire, first in its physical and then in its verbal aspect, is the motivating force behind that episode which most clearly highlights the nature of narrative in the *1001 Nights.*

In his discussion of *Beyond the Pleasure Principle* in "Freud's Masterplot," Peter Brooks repeatedly remarks the significance of desire as a concept in the development of any narrative. "Any reflection on novelistic beginnings," notes Brooks, "shows the beginning as an awakening, an arousal, the birth of an appetency, ambition, desire, or intention."[11] The action of the frame story and of the interlude in particular underscores this point. The arousal of the porter's sexual desires corresponds to his awakening interest in the kind of narrative possible within the women's realm. The porter is ultimately incapable of creatively concretizing this interest; his narrative offering is forgettable at best. But it is his larger narrative interest, his desire to hear the narratives of his cohorts, that helps to propel the cycle on its proper course.

His own desire for narrative is subsidiary to the women's desire, which, in its turn, is instigated by the communal narrative desire of their guests. "Desire," remarks Brooks, "must be considered the very motor of narrative, its dynamic principle."[12] And indeed, it is the very basic desire to know why something happened and what happens next that drives the story of the porter and the three ladies forward. The porter, as always, best articulates the questioning that prompts the initial impulse toward narrative: "The porter approached her and said, 'My lady, these men express the wish that you acquaint them with the story of the two black bitches and why you punish them and then weep over them, and they wish to know the story of your sister and how it was that she got flogged with the whip, like a man. That is all; that is what they want to know'" (84).[13] The porter's request addresses the most fundamental of narrative issues: how a story moves from beginning to end. What, he asks, are the incidents that have led to this final state? What is the story that accounts for this ending? The pertinent suggestion is that the desire for narrative is nothing other than the desire for the completion and coherence that are obtained by following the manipulations of plot through to their final point.

There are, of course, as many ways of arriving at this final point as there are stories to tell. Certain conditions of narrative development must obtain, however, for the very nature of narrative demands adherence to those laws of composition that distinguish it from other literary forms. The most fundamental of these laws is that of succession, the movement from one event to another. "Où il n'y a pas succession," remarks Claude Brémond, "il n'y a pas récit."[14] One event must follow another. Narrative cannot be static; it must progress along a continuum, move forward, unfold in time. Conventional narrative requires a connection between one event and its successor, a logical or causal connection that ensures the coherence needed to determine a narrative sequence. It is, according to Roland Barthes, the practical application of the logical error: *post hoc ergo propter hoc*.[15]

This narrative succession and consequence constitute what is usually described as the linearity of narrative. The continuum along which narrative events progress or unfold provides the line that defines the plot of the narrative. The relation that subsists among the individual members of this series is generally agreed to be one of contiguity. Events progress horizontally along an axis that has both spatial and temporal coordinates. And in his now classic formulation, Roman Jakobson identifies this association by contiguity as the fundamental impulse behind prose narrative and thus establishes a connection between prose and metonymy. It is no accident that Peter Brooks, following Lacan, has equated metonymy, that figure of contiguity and forward movement, with desire, the driving power of narrative.

III

One must not forget the lesson of the interlude, however. In that part of the narrative that tells most openly about the role of desire in the cycle of the three ladies in particular and in the *1001 Nights* in general, metonymy is not foregrounded as the primary movement of narrative progression. It is metaphor that is associated not only with desire but with the dominant movement of narrative within the work as well. If the metonymic impulse of narrative encourages its author to move forward "from the plot to the atmosphere and from the characters to the setting in space and time,"[16] metaphor generates the narrative sphere in which an objective, referential connection between a word and a thing, between a thing and its neighbor, does not apply. Why, then, this metaphoric deviance in a work that stands as a paragon of prose narrative art? Is the *1001 Nights* subverting the basic impulse of narrative? Or is it trying to tell us something about the relation between metaphor and a specific kind of narrative discourse?

In fact, neither Jakobson nor Brooks ignores the potential of metaphor as a structuring compositional device for prose. If Jakobson associates metaphor primarily with poetry, he does allow that no poetic discourse relies solely on metaphor, just as no prose discourse relies solely on metonymy.[17] Brooks takes this necessary connection further.

47

If narrative progresses by virtue of the contiguous relations of its individual parts, metaphor stands as a figurative expression for the way the beginning of a narrative is connected to its subsequent middle and end. Brooks derives his explanation of this metaphoric structure from Todorov's analysis of narrative development in his article entitled "Les transformations narratives":

> Todorov elaborates a model of narrative transformation whereby narrative plot (*le récit*) is constituted in the tension of two formal categories, difference and resemblance. Transformation—a change in a predicate term common to beginning and end—represents a synthesis of difference and resemblance; it is, we might say, the same-but-different. Now the "same-but-different" is a common . . . definition of metaphor. . . . Narrative operates as metaphor in its affirmation of resemblance, in that it brings into relation different actions, combines them through perceived similarities (Todorov's common predicate term), appropriates them to a common plot, which implies the rejection of merely contingent (or unassimilable) incident or action. The plotting of meaning cannot do without metaphor, for meaning in plot is the structure of action in closed and legible wholes. Metaphor is in this sense totalizing.[18]

The metaphoric structure binds the plot, provides the initial and final limits within which the narrative metonymically unfolds, ensures the relation of resemblance that must subsist among individual narrative segments. If, as Todorov asserts, narrative lies in the movement between two states that, though different, are connected in their resemblance, the metaphoric structure of narrative lies in the process by which an initial term is transformed into a second term that, by virtue of its similarity, replaces it. The metonymic chain of plot is enclosed within the metaphoric limits of the narrative.

However, without the movement instigated by the metonymic drive, metaphor would collapse into the static condition contained in a completed metaphor, one in which the second term has already subsumed the first. It is, as both Brooks and Jakobson repeatedly remark, the metonymic impulse that ensures the temporal expansion necessary for the achievement of narrative, while the structure of metaphor provides the outer limits within which this achievement can occur. Inevitably, a tension between the two figures subsists. Metonymy is the forward-moving figure of contiguity, of linearity. In its tracing of the horizontal axis, it participates in the syntagmatic plan of discourse, which differentially defines the movement of all significant speech. Metaphor, by contrast, belongs to the order of paradigm, which falls out along a vertical axis. Instead of following the continuum that corresponds to the necessary syntactic sequence of both speech and narrative, metaphor operates largely on the basis of substitution and similarity. A word does not mean metaphorically by virtue of its syntactic opposition to another word, but rather by virtue of its capacity to resemble, indeed repeat in different guise, the term it replaces. Metaphoric discourse, then, does not in the main proceed sequentially through time as does its metonymic counterpart. Instead it turns back upon itself in an effort to maintain its static position.

In "La quête du récit," Todorov isolates two types of narrative ordeal in the medieval romance *The Quest of the Holy Grail:* the narrative and the ritual.[19] In the first type, the hero engages in a series of adventures whose outcome is unspecified at the outset. The reader shadows the protagonist's activities, follows the movement of the narrative, in the interest of discovering what happens next and how it all will end. The second type of ordeal does not allow for the same kind of narrative suspense. Here all is predetermined from the start. What matters is not the action and outcome of the sequence, for that is already known by the reader, but rather the undertaking of the act, the rite of (often narrative) passage that is signified in the accomplishment of the act. Each of these ordeals is associated with a particular and primary form of narrative structure and organization. The first unfolds along the horizontal axis and allows one event to follow another in strict narrative succession. It is, according to Todorov, a narrative of contiguity, and the technique of plot combination that supports it is linking (*enchaînement*). The second type of narrative structure is based upon a series of variations whose relations are vertically determined. Ritual can—indeed, must—be endlessly repeatable. Its affiliation, then, is with a narrative of substitution that is built upon so many repetitions. The compositional technique that corresponds here is embedding (*enchâssement*).

The tropic equivalents of these two types of narrative structure are clearly metonymy and metaphor, and Todorov accordingly associates the two organizational paradigms with prose and poetry, respectively. The correspondence between the narrative structure of ritual and the *1001 Nights* in general and the cycle of "The Porter and the Three Ladies" in particular is immediately obvious. There is clearly an alliance here with the compositional and structural elements that define the narrative of ritual. The first of these is clearly the interlude's insistence on metaphor and metaphoric structures. Closely related to this is the ritualistic character of the interlude itself.

IV

The reader can easily detect in the interlude of "The Porter and the Three Ladies" a narrative aspect that immediately sets it apart from the preceding sequence. Indeed, it is this aspect that allows one to qualify the passage describing the porter's initiation into the private realm of the three ladies as an interlude, a period of respite from the narrative activity that precedes and follows this moment of seemingly insignificant play. If one accepts the conventional definition of ritual as a form of customary behavior, of patterned activity,

with a primarily symbolic, nonempirical referent, the interlude can be read as a ritualistic act whose purpose is to communicate a linguistic system that is itself symbolically, in this
case metaphorically, based.

As in all ritualistic behavior, the aesthetic aspect of the
act is particularly prominent, a prominence that is achieved
and even heightened in the predictable, and therefore repeatable, action or series of actions that make up the rite.
The activity of the interlude makes the point. The first lady,
the doorkeeper, establishes the procedure that her two sisters and, eventually, the porter will follow. The ritual can be
broken down into twelve discrete units, which are generally
introduced by the conjunction *wa,* "and," *thumma,* "then," or
fa, "and" or "so." In its barest narrative outlines, the initial
series of actions is presented in the following way: (1) the
doorkeeper went to the pool, (2) and she took off all her
clothes; (3) then she threw herself into the pool; (4) then she
washed herself; (5) then she emerged from the water, (6) and
she threw herself into the lap of the porter, (7) and she said
to him, "My lord and my love, what is this?" (8) and she
pointed to her slit; (9) and the porter said, "Your womb,"
(10) and she started hitting him; (11) then he said to her, "All
right, what is its name?" (12) and the naked girl replied,
"The basil of the bridges."

This provides an almost unalterable and unvarying pattern for the events that follow. The second lady takes her cue
from her predecessor, and in her turn reiterates, in a slightly
abbreviated narrative form, the ritual activity. As the narrator points out in the opening line of the sequence, she acts in
this capacity "like her sister," mimicking her actions and even
her language exactly. The only alteration she effects in the
pattern is that upon emerging from the pool, she clothes
herself. The ritualistic aspect of this feminine ceremony is
paradoxically underscored by this slight variation in the pattern that has been so carefully established.

The third lady's performance is, in narrative terms,

perfunctory—a lack compensated for by a rather more elaborate description of the woman's naked body and the porter's poetic response to it. The third lady does indeed fulfill the necessary sequence of events, but the narrator has at this point seemingly lost interest in embellishing her actions and consequently presents them in brief, almost resumptive form. "To make a long story short, O King," says Shahrazad, to explain why she passes over the direct speech of the porter, in fear, perhaps, that the king himself is not susceptible to the charms of repetition. And yet the pattern at this point has been so well established that it remains stable despite such editing.

It is the porter who inherits this ritualistic legacy, although he cannot ultimately incorporate the symbolic code communicated by the ritual into his linguistic realm. In participating in the ceremony, however, he makes manifest the necessary transmissible aspect of all ritual, its capacity to transcend temporal, spatial, and sexual boundaries, and to be thereby transferred from one generation to another. The porter repeats the ritual in exactly the same sequence established by the ladies; and although their responses differ from his own in their playful aspect—they are, after all, the masters, as it were, of these ritualistic gestures—his careful repetition of the correct actions signals his entry into the closed society of the women.

I noted earlier that the porter's fundamental insecurity and ultimate failure within this special realm are reflected in his exact repetition of and dependence upon the nominative expressions offered by the three women. However, it is at the same time in this very repetition, this insistent enclosure within a prescribed realm, that the ritualistic aspect of the sequence is underscored. In admitting only those terms sanctioned by the women, the porter can be seen as maintaining the sequence established by feminine tradition and thereby preserving ritual sanctity. The formal pattern of the porter's formulation further emphasizes this repetitive aspect. Not only does he carefully repeat the nominal hierarchy of the sequence—the smashing mule grazes in the basil of the bridges of the first lady, eats the second lady's husked sesame, and gallops in the third lady's inn—but the rhythmical and rhyming patterns within the phrase (al-baghl al-ka*sūr* yar'ā ḥabaq al-ju*sūr* wa-yasuffu al-simsim al-maq*shūr* wa-yubarṭi'u fī khān abū mas*rūr*) attest to the fundamentally repetitive structure and self-referential aspect of the sequence.

Indeed, the ritualistic repetition of the interlude as a whole is not limited to its gestural fabric alone but is mirrored in the verbal fabric of the passage. Instead of varying the language used to describe the repeated sequence of events, the narrator generally uses the same words and phrases. One could invoke the Parry/Lord theory of oral formulaic composition as described in *The Singer of Tales* and argue that such repetition is the result of the techniques necessitated by the demands of oral composition, that the narrator has a bag of formulas and themes that he or she can pull out and work into the tale in order to move the narrative along.[20] But there is a self-consciousness in the three ladies interlude that suggests a fundamental awareness of the repetitive narrative technique being employed. Not only does the narrator carefully establish the consequent change in subject (while maintaining the same verb) each time the ritual series is repeated, thereby indicating an awareness that the same is being perpetuated with only a slight difference; but she (this is, after all, Shahrazad narrating) uses phrases such as "like her sister" or "to make a long story short," which suggest a strong narrative consciousness vis-à-vis the repetitive aspect of the sequence. Similarly, the repeated words, sounds, and rhythms of the porter's expression linguistically simulate his gestural repetition of the women's actions. In short, what is said and done within the ritual of the interlude can only reiterate what has already been said and done. Ultimately, the significance of the activity lies in its very capacity to be repeated and to be thereby ritually and ritualistically continued.

What, finally, is the relation between this narrative of ritual, this ritual narrative, and the trope with which it is affiliated? Why do the women choose to teach the porter about metaphor by engaging in a ritualistically arranged sequence of events? Why does Todorov for his part identify the structure of ritual ordeal with the figure of metaphor? The answer lies in part in the resemblance between the movement which the larger outlines of each describe, in their mutual dependence on the backward-turning movement of repetition. For if the ritual activity of the interlude is premised upon its repetition of initially posited verbal and gestural patterns, metaphor too is premised upon the capacity of the second term to repeat the first. Indeed, the meaning of a metaphor lies largely in this repetition, in the likeness between one meaning and its transported, metaphorical one, in Aristotle's renowned perception of the similarity in dissimilars.

One cannot, however, posit repetition without simultaneously positing difference. No action, no matter how carefully imitated, can ever exactly repeat its precursor, for the very fact of its imitation, its repetition, necessitates its occurring at a different moment and, consequently, its having a different status. I remarked above, for example, that the fully ritualistic, repetitive aspect of the interlude was brought home in the moment it announced its difference from the preceding sequences, which it otherwise carefully imitated. Metaphoric movement and meaning exemplify the issue even more clearly. The similarity perceived in dissimilars relies upon the relation of difference and distance as well as of resemblance and proximity between the two terms of the metaphor. The second term can repeat the first only because it is different from it; if it were not, the first term could never be metaphorically extended but would exist within its immediately referential parameters. There are, certainly, degrees of metaphoric difference; the second term can resemble the first to a greater or lesser extent. The three women proclaim a metaphorization in which the two terms are only opaquely similar, in Walter Benjamin's phrase, in which little obvious connection subsists between the literal name and its metaphoric replacement.[21] There is a greater distance to travel between the first term and the second, in part, as I suggested earlier, because the women are establishing a language that operates largely according to their own gendered distinctions; but also in part because metaphor is, in this instance, occupying the territory more often inhabited by metonymy. The prosaic succession normally instigated by metonymy is thus figuratively replaced by the metaphoric distance one must travel between the two terms.

Regardless of this distance and corresponding differential tension, though, the fundamental movement of metaphor remains the same. No matter how far one must travel in order to make the correspondence between the two terms, one must always turn back in order to replace, repeat, the first term with the second. It is unavoidable, even inevitable, that a narrative predominantly affiliated with and generated by ritual structure and metaphoric figures move differently from one that follows the metonymic course. I would suggest that it is to the status and function of repetition as a kind of narrative structure and movement that one should look for this essential difference.

V

Repetition has long been recognized as a fundamental structuring device for poetry and has been posited as the formal basis for the poetic act. Gerard Manley Hopkins's definition of verse as "speech wholly or partially repeating the same figure of sound" points to the basic premise underlying this attitude. Poetry is a system traditionally built on repetition and, associatively, parallelism. The regular alliteration of comparable metrical phenomena organizes poetry into a series of parallel lines that mirror each other rhythmically; while the potential for the repeated sounds of rhyme, or of other verbal devices such as assonance and alliteration, can contribute to the poetic fabric woven of repeated and repeatable structures. In his seminal discussions on the formal characteristics of poetry, Jakobson again and again underlines the centrality of repetition and similarity in organizing poetic discourse. In the now-classic "Two Aspects of Language," he writes: "The principle of similarity underlies poetry; the metrical parallelism of lines or the phonic equivalence of rhyming words prompts the question of semantic similarity and contrast."[22] Or in a later essay: "The repetitiveness effected by imparting the equivalence principle to the sequence makes reiterable not only the constituent sequences of the poetic message but the whole message as well. This capacity for reiteration whether immediate or delayed, this conversion of a message into an enduring thing, indeed all this represents an inherent and effective property of poetry."[23] It is this necessary capacity for parallel and repeatable sequences that defines not only the poetic structure but the poetic message as well. The accommodating trope is metaphor.

Theorists of prose have until recently been less ready to admit the value of repetition as a potential structuring device of prose narrative and have generally deemed any repetitive sequence or structure as pejoratively repetitious. The largely linear, metonymic fashion in which prose theoretically progresses in the main wards off the backward turnings of repetition, necessitates that the narrative unfold with an eye to the future, which is the end, rather than to the past, which was the beginning. In "sophisticated" prose narrative, accordingly, there are, or at least should be, no significant repetitions. "Primitive" narrative is exempt from this claim. As the anthropologist Franz Boas noted in his early work on primitive art: "The investigation of primitive narrative as well as of poetry proves that repetition, particularly rhythmic repetition, is one of its fundamental, esthetic traits."[24]

To some extent, it is often the presence of such generally obvious and wholesale repetitions that allows one to qualify a text as "primitive." Folk literature is particularly susceptible to this charge. Snow White encounters seven dwarfs, and later dies and is resurrected three times in succession; the five brothers of Boas's Chinook Indian tale have the same adventure one right after the other; King Shahrayar experiences, in heightened fashion, the same betrayal as his brother King Shahzaman. As Gérard Genette remarks in his discussion of repetition as a narrative structuring device: "Un événement n'est pas seulement capable de se produire: il peut aussi se reproduire, ou se répéter: le soleil se lève tous les jours."[25] In the *1001 Nights* the same sun sets every night.

Chapter Four

Once More for Emphasis
Patterns of Narrative Repetition

The Prince of the Believers, 'Alī ibn Abī Ṭālib—May God
be pleased with him!—has said, "Were discourse not repeated, it would dwindle away." . . . Someone [else] has
said, "Anything you repeat is shortened, except discourse:
if you repeat it, it grows."
                            —al-ʿAskarī, *Kitāb al-Ṣināʿatayn*

I

THE *1001 Nights* is premised upon a fundamental act of
repetition. Not only is Shahrazad's narrative and sexual
activity repeated nightly; it also results in the perpetuation of
Shahrayar's royal line, his extension, his repetition of himself
in time through his progeny.[1] The frame story of the three
ladies plays with the same notion in its foregrounding of the
ritualistically repetitive verbal and genital play and potential
generative activity. But the way in which repetitive structures
are elaborated in "The Porter and the Three Ladies" extends
much further and is far more complicated.

In one of the earliest discussions of narrative repetition,
Gérard Genette lays the ground rules for a discussion of

what constitutes repetition in prose narrative. Once one has posited that an event can happen again, that the sun rises every morning, remarks Genette, one must also posit that the exact identity of these recurring events is debatable:

> La "répétition" est en fait une construction de l'esprit, qui élimine de chaque occurrence tout ce qui lui appartient en propre pour n'en conserver que ce qu'elle partage avec toutes les autres de la même classe, et qui est une abstraction: . . . Cela est bien connu, et je ne le rappelle que pour préciser une fois pour toutes que l'on nommera ici "événements identiques" ou "récurrence du même événement" une série de plusieurs événements semblables et *considérés dans leur seule ressemblance.*[2]

Genette's point is well taken and has, of course, been made most famously in Saussure's discussion of the Paris-Geneva 8:45 P.M. express. There is, can be, no repetition without difference, no exact identity between events, simply because any event that is repeated necessarily occurs at a time later than that of the initial, original event. What Genette is here hinting at is the almost genetic relationship between repetition and time, the fact that repetition has no significant meaning without the temporal dimension. I shall consider this connection at length in a later discussion. For the moment, let us remember that what one considers in an examination of narrative repetition is the larger correspondences within the text, the significantly similar though not exact textual recurrences that to a greater or lesser degree make the text cohere.

These larger correspondences, these recurring textual events, generally occur on the story level of the narrative, the plane on which the narrative sequence of events unfolds. These events can mirror one another in their larger structure. One incident can recall the broader outlines of an earlier one, just as the significant pattern of a particular sequence or episode can recur throughout a narrative. But the scale of such repetitions can be reduced and individual aspects of a complex unit can offer themselves for replication, if not multiplication, in the course of a narrative. Thus, the recurrence of a particular motif that in its larger capacity signals in fuguelike fashion one of possibly multiple leitmotivs within a narrative; or similarly, the doubling, or more often trebling, of a character within a story; and finally, the repetition of a particular action or gesture. As Susan Suleiman points out in her chapter on textual redundancy in *Authoritarian Fictions*, these individual story repetitions can be manipulated in a variety of ways: the same event can happen to a number of different characters; or alternatively, the same event can repeatedly happen to the same character; or finally, the same event can happen to different characters who are, fundamentally, replicas of one another.[3] The harmonious playing of all these potential story variations occurs within any given narrative of the *1001 Nights*.

But if an event or motif or character or action occurs within a narrative, it must somehow manifest itself in the verbal fabric of a story, on the level of the story's discourse. There are, again, narrative alternatives, for a narrative aspect or element that recurs within a text need not, obviously, be repeatedly presented via the same verbal machinery. Indeed, such repetitions in seemingly "sophisticated" narratives are as often as not cloaked in different verbal guises in order to preserve something resembling a forward narrative movement. In some instances—as in the ritualistic naming scene in the three ladies frame story—the same character, event, or context receives the same verbal commentary each time it occurs. There are in addition, however, verbal repetitions that are, in a fashion, detached from the story level of the narrative, moments of evaluation, commentary, or reflection on the part of either the narrator or a character which recur at significant points throughout a text. At a further level of narrative remove, these wholesale verbal repetitions serve as narrative markers within the text, linguistic devices to indicate to the reader or listener that he or she is still moving within a narrative universe. Again, all of these verbal strains sound variously and with variation in specific cycles of the *1001 Nights*.

These different aspects of narrative repetition can be variously named and interpreted. Shlomith Rimmon-Kenan, citing Jean Cohen, distinguishes between the repetition of a sign: "a retelling of an event in the *récit* in exactly the same words, by the same narrator, with the same focalisation"; the signifier: "[the use of] the same discourse (i.e. *récit*) elements to narrate different *histoire*-events"; and finally, the signified: the repetition of the "same *histoire*-event using different discourse-elements."[4] J. Hillis Miller further categorizes the nature of the relations between fiction and repetition. Not only are there those repetitions which help to create the structure of the work within itself; but there are in addition those repetitions which operate between the text and what exists outside its immediate textual domain: "the author's mind or his life; other works by the same author; psychological, social, or historical reality; other works by other authors; motifs from the mythological or fabulous past; elements from the purported past of the characters or of their ancestors; events which have occurred before the book begins."[5] Miller goes on to qualify the difference among potential structures of repetition. Citing Gilles Deleuze in *Logique du sens*, he distinguishes between "Platonic repetition," those repeated structures which derive from a solid, archetypal model of the world and therefore participate in obvious and immediate similarities or identities, and the "Nietzschean mode of repetition," which posits a world based solely on difference, in which each thing can only vaguely, opaquely, darkly repeat or resemble another.[6] Day versus night, icon versus phantasm, repetition versus difference: ultimately, it depends upon the individual text to manipulate the various possibilities.

There is another aspect of narrative repetition that has

not yet been considered, an aspect in which all narrative, arguably all linguistic, structures participate. In this view, a narrative is not only the locus for different modes of repetition, the forum within which various repetitions occur, but it is itself the fundamental repetition of the text; it is intrinsically a kind of repetition, a restating, retelling, recapitulation of events or states that have existed prior to their being narratively transmuted. In this light, the narrative act itself becomes the task of the translator. As Genette notes in a recent essay: "Concurrence ou traduction, la simulation réaliste est encore, ou déjà, variation sur ce même thème obligé, c'est-à-dire convenue, qu'on appelle Histoire, société, vérité, bonheur, Temps perdu, que sais-je encore, et que la représentation la plus 'fidèle' nous invite, non sans détours, à *ricercare.*"[7]

One might rightly argue that this attitude of narrative as a fundamental act of repetition applies only to mimetic narratives in which, following Deleuze's Platonic model of daylight repetition, the narrative clearly imitates, mirrors, repeats an antecedent, exterior presence. But all literary narrative, after all, locates itself in language, derives its essence from that linguistic element which gives it voice. Following Saussure, one might argue that the sign is itself a repetition, in this case an opaquely similar one, of the thing it signifies; and further, that signs can function meaningfully within the linguistic system only because they can be repeated. As one critic remarks, "Only because a spoken element repeats or conforms to an essentially repeatable form can it be recognized as language. A person recognizes a word or a sentence as such because he or she re-cognizes its form, that is, re-members its past repetitions."[8]

In this light, no text escapes the pressure of repetition. Any linguistic utterance, regardless of intention or scope, must submit to the determining restrictions of a repetitive mode. But so pervasive, so fundamental is repetition in our use and experience of linguistic and literary structures that

we are tempted to accept the matter as given, if not insignificant, and to pursue its consequences no further. If all verbal
utterances function according to the same basic mode, why
exaggerate the importance of this aspect in a particular
work? Why not read it with the same assumptions, the same
attitudes one brings to any text? The answer lies, naturally,
in the fact that any work can emphasize and manipulate its
repetitive scaffolding to a greater or lesser extent. When
Peter Brooks talks about the connection between different
moments in a text, the metaphoric progression of the "same-
but-different" elements along the metonymic line of the text,
he is talking about the necessary interconnection, repetition
of certain basic textual elements that bind a particular text,
make it cohere, and allow the reader to distinguish one work
from another. This kind of repetition is basic to any
narrative—Homeric epic depends upon it as much as a novel
by Flaubert—and thus resists any interpretation that reads
repetition as a thing out of the ordinary, a counter to or
subversion of the metonymic impulse of prose. I would argue that the cycle of "The Porter and the Three Ladies," by
contrast, consciously manipulates its repetitive underpinnings, plays with them, mirrors and mocks them, so that
even the reader who is not particularly sensitive to such manipulation is forced to come to terms with its significance.

II

The sequence of "The Porter and the Three Ladies" is one
of the most intricate cycles of tales within the *1001 Nights*.
Various structures, motifs, voices, and phrases are articu-
lated at the outset of the cycle only to be developed and
replayed either in exactly the same way or in a slightly altered fashion. To some extent, the tales in the cycle seem to
be nothing more than variations on a theme. Echoes sound
and re-sound. With each new story, we sense that we have

heard all this before, and indeed we have. Repetition is central to the development of the cycle, for it constitutes the basic structural pattern of the major tales. It is, however, in the tales of the three dervishes in particular that the reader is most urgently forced to acknowledge the value of repetition as a narrative structuring device. What follows is an attempt to outline the various patterns of repetition within these tales in their different contexts.

One should begin at the beginning, in this case, outside the text, and remember that the earliest version of the *1001 Nights* was an aurally intended work performed before a live audience. André Miquel notes that it was possibly told as part of the *samar,* "cette pratique quasi institutionnêlle de la culture arabo-musulmane classique: la conversation nocturne. . . . Le *samar* est d'ordinaire ce qui clôt la journée active, avant le repos nocturne, et l'on a toutes raisons de penser que c'est de ce type-là que relève le *samar* du conteur, qu'on l'imagine au milieu d'un groupe restreint ou sur la place publique."[9] The storyteller nightly tells his story about a woman who nightly tells her stories and who, like him, depends upon the approval of her audience in order to continue the narrative act and, ultimately, in order to stay alive. The pattern persists. In the three ladies cycle, the primary narrative-men, the three dervishes, repeat this narrative act and they too tell their stories to avoid death. Eventually the narrative burden is transferred to two of the three women who asymmetrically bring the cycle to a successful close.

To a certain extent, this repetition of the narrative act is a function of the embedding/embedded cycle structure, but the pattern is repeated within the individual tales themselves. The frame story, as always, suggests the incipient pattern. The doorkeeper announces each new arrival by giving her sisters a brief history of the strangers. All we know initially about the three dervishes is what the doorkeeper tells us via her sisters. The caliph's case, as noted earlier, is somewhat different. We first hear the caliph's story indirectly, as it were. The first-person voice interrupts the narrative: "Now the cause of that knocking, O King, was . . . " and goes on to explain Harun al-Rashid's situation. Thus, the reader receives information that the principle characters within the tale do not, so that the narrative can continue to unroll unimpeded. Ja'far then assumes the narrative voice and presents the fictionalized account of the caliph et al. to the doorkeeper: "O my lady, we are merchants from the city of Mosul. . . ." There is consequently no need, narratively speaking, for the doorkeeper to repeat the stories directly, as she did in the case of the three dervishes. It is enough to be told that "she went back to her sisters and repeated Ja'far's story to them." Regardless of how it is done, though, the story—the complete story (this is perhaps one reason why the caliph has no story to tell; Shahrazad has told it for him)—is told. In the frame story itself, the power of narrative has taken hold.

Once within the individual tales, the narrative act continues to be repeated, to mirror itself; and true to the model established by Shahrazad, the connection between narrative and death remains constant, although subject to variation. In each of the dervish's tales, one plot-significant story within the story, always preceded by the predicate *qāla/qālat*, "he/she said," is told. In the first tale, the dervish's uncle relates the story of the incestuous relationship between his daughter and his son: "Nephew, you should know that this son of mine was madly in love with his sister, and I often forbade him from seeing her but went on saying to myself, 'They are only children'" (90).[10] This narrative does not, of course, forestall death but rather explains in a minor key the death of the dervish's cousin and his mysterious companion.

The second dervish's tale follows this established pattern. In response to the dervish's account of his own history, the beautiful woman narrates the story of her imprisonment: "Then I related to her my mishaps, and she felt sad for me and said, 'I too shall tell you my tale'" (96).[11] Again, the narrative/death connection is altered. In this case, far from escaping death, the woman's story indirectly causes her own demise, for the secrets she divulges allow the dervish to summon the jinn.

The pattern persists and the theme is varied yet again in the third dervish's tale. Here the embedded narrative of the young boy explains another seemingly bizarre imprisonment. At the request of the dervish, the prisoner explains his situation: "My lady, when I asked the young man to tell me his story, and he was assured that I was of his kind, he rejoiced and regained his composure. Then he made me draw near to him and said, 'O my brother, my case is strange and my tale is amazing'" (118).[12] One expects that this time, at least, narrative will succeed in altering the narrator's fated death, that once informed of destiny's possible course, the dervish will take special pains to avoid it. But fully forewarned, he fulfills the narrative's predictions by killing his underground companion. Once again, the power of narrative has failed.

By the time the three dervishes reach Baghdad, however, they are apparently sufficiently acquainted with the destructive force of narrative to eschew its negative powers. As primary, embedding storytellers, they follow Shahrazad's lead in manipulating the life-giving potential of narrative. The garrulous dervishes need only the incentive manifested in the command that closes the frame story to tell their stories. They have clearly learned the power of narrative and are consequently wise and proficient in the art of storytelling. Their tales ensue and death is forestalled.

It would seem that the three dervishes have learned their art from the same master, for each of their tales harmonizes the same notes in different keys. One might expect as much, since all three dervishes share significant physical characteristics. The doorkeeper insists upon this strange coincidence: "At this very moment, three one-eyed dervishes are standing at the door, each with a shaven head, shaven beard, and shaven eyebrows, and each blind in the right eye. It is a most amazing coincidence" (76).[13] And later the caliph himself remarks such unusual similarity with equal astonishment. With such priming, one expects a certain congruence in the three tales to be told. We are not disappointed.

One cannot, needless to say, reduce the three dervishes' stories to a simple scheme. To do so would be to disregard the art of storytelling, which is of the utmost importance here. The three dervishes' safety implicitly depends, after all, on the pleasing quality of their narratives. But there are certain invariants common to all three tales which combine to form the foundation on which the stories are built. Each dervish begins his story by genealogically identifying himself, by implicitly disavowing his pose as a dervish for his rightful royal persona. "My father was a king," remarks the first dervish, "and he had a brother who was also a king" (86).[14] The second dervish similarly prefaces his story. "My father was a king, and he taught me how to write and read," he notes (92).[15] The third dervish, curiously, disclaims any potential similarity to his two predecessors: "O great lady, the story behind the shaving off of my beard and the loss of my eye is stranger and more amazing than theirs, yet it is unlike theirs, for their misfortune took them by surprise, whereas I knowingly brought misfortune and sorrow upon myself" (114).[16] And yet he immediately belies his own assertion and remarks, "My father was a great and powerful king" (114).[17] Once again, difference underscores repetition. The initial parallels have been established.

Once this initial coincidence of physical characteristic and lineage has been asserted, the stories proceed in broadly similar lines. At the opening of each story, the king has journeyed from his court on a mission of largely personal interest and importance. The first dervish sets out to visit a cousin to whom he is bound by a "firm friendship and a great affection." (In the Bulaq edition they share the same birth

date.) The second dervish embarks on a journey of undoubtedly but not dominantly diplomatic import to the king of
India in order to display his intellectual talents; while the
third dervish engages in Sindbadlike fashion on a voyage of
exploration to some nearby islands. During this absence
from court, a disturbance of either a political (the overthrow
of the first dervish's government), social (the waylaying of
the second dervish by highway men), or natural (the third
dervish's shipwreck) order occurs and results in a loss of
station and prolonged exile. At some generally early point in
the journey that follows this disturbance, each dervish encounters a richly furnished underground prison or hideaway
whose inhabitants are ultimately destroyed by the unwitting
offices of the dervish. The first dervish's adventures come to
a close at this point, but the second and third dervishes press
on in a fashion that has been radically influenced by their
underground encounter. All three eventually make their
way to Baghdad, and it is in this city of the three women that
each meets his brother in misfortune.

Just as the dervishes' introductory statements echoed
each other, so do the endings to their stories. Each dervish
specifies his intention to travel to Baghdad (though only the
first two indicate their desire to tell their story to the caliph);
each affirms his status as a stranger, an outsider in the city;
and each indicates, either implicitly or explicitly, his alliance
with his two fellow travelers. The first dervish describes the
scene in the following way:

> Then I left the city, undetected by anyone, and journeyed
> to this country, with the intention of reaching Baghdad,
> hoping that I might be fortunate to find someone who
> would assist me to the presence of the Commander of the
> Faithful, the Vice Regent of the Supreme Lord, so that I
> might tell him my tale and lay my case before him. I ar-
> rived this very night, and as I stood in doubt at the city
> gate, not knowing where I should go, this dervish by my
> side approached me, showing the signs of travel, and

greeted me. I asked him, "Are you a stranger?" and when he replied, "Yes," I said, "I too am a stranger." As we were talking, this other dervish by our side joined us at the gate, greeted us, and said, "I am a stranger." We replied, "We are strangers too." Then the three of us walked as night overtook us, three strangers who did not know where to go. (91)[18]

The second dervish has clearly taken his cue from the first. With little interest in narrative or stylistic variation, he confirms their encounter by repeating his brother's description:

Then I journeyed through many regions and visited many countries, with the intention of reaching Baghdad and the hope of finding someone there who would help me to the presence of the Commander of the Faithful, so that I might tell him my tale and acquaint him with my misfortune. I arrived here this very night and found this man my brother standing about. I greeted him and asked, "Are you a stranger?" and he replied, "Yes, I am a stranger." Soon this other man joined us and said, "I am a stranger," and we replied, "We too are strangers like you." Then the three of us walked on, as night descended on us, until God brought us to your house. (113)[19]

The third dervish, true not only to his form but to the narrative form established in the ritual naming scene of the frame story, abbreviates his account of the final encounter. Dismissing any interest in relating his story to the caliph and avoiding any unnecessary modifying phrases or dialogue, the third dervish describes only the essentials of the scene:

Then God granted me safe passage and I reached Baghdad on the evening of this very night. Here I met these two men standing at a loss, and I greeted them and said, "I am a stranger," and they replied, "We are strangers like you." We formed an extraordinary group, for by coincidence, all three of us happened to be blind in the right eye. (132)[20]

One immediately notices the repetition of phrases, of qualifiers, of attitudes among the three descriptions. Not only does there seem to be uniform agreement as to what happened when the three dervishes met, but there is also a striking coincidence in the way this meeting is described. Equally noteworthy, though, are the parallels, the repetitions within the individual accounts. The first dervish's pose is mirrored by the second; both the second and the third dervishes appear to the first with equal suddenness; and all three verbally identify in exact fashion their status as strangers, indeed, make a point of underscoring this coincidence: "I *too* am a stranger." Thus the repeated attempts to distinguish one dervish from the other: "this dervish by my side" or "the other dervish."

Also worth noticing is the manner in which the three seemingly set pieces of narration insist on their coincidence and potential for difference. Each of the dervishes emphasizes that each was a stranger to the others until quite recently and therefore ignorant of the others' story. As the third dervish remarks, "We formed an extraordinary group, for by coincidence, all three of us happened to be blind in the right eye." The point is clear. What the dervishes are doing is remarking the surprising coincidence among not only their persons but their stories as well, and assuring their audience that such a coincidence is both purely fortuitous and worthy of special attention. We didn't prearrange such congruence, suggest the first two dervishes; it happened to us just by chance, reassures the third. Once again, narrative difference underscores narrative repetition.

Each tale, then, shares a common narrative situation, but each storyteller naturally makes different use of it, develops his tale differently. The first dervish's tale is told simply, without recourse to otherworldly elements or excessive rhetorical devices, while the second and third dervishes' tales become increasingly fantastic and tropically elaborate. This stylistic progression from first to third tale is paralleled in the narrative development of the individual tales. The first dervish's story constitutes what Roland Barthes calls a single cardinal function; it unfolds along a single, uninterrupted narrative line that traces the history and consequences of the dervish's visit to his uncle and cousin. The second dervish's tale appropriately follows two separate though related functions. The first of these describes his adventures from the time of his journey to the king of India to his transformation into an ape; while the second details his history from the point of this transformation to its reversal. The third dervish takes this narrative development one step further. The first narrative sequence follows the dervish through to his underground adventures with the young boy; the second focuses on his encounter with the ten repentant men who are blind in one eye; and the third and most elaborate sequence finally describes his relations with the forty beautiful women of the magic castle.

Inevitably, new elements and situations are introduced in each succeeding narrative in order to accommodate the ever-expanding scope; yet despite their novelty, it always seems as if we have encountered them before. The series of rapid metamorphoses that occur at the end of the second dervish's tale, for example, replay in highly ornamental fashion the earlier metamorphosis of the same dervish into an ape. The deep-black horse saddled with red gold behind the forbidden door of the castle recalls the brass horseman of Magnet Mountain in the third dervish's tale. Such echoes sound not only within the individual tales but among the tales as a larger unit. Thus the magic words traced by the king's daughter in the second tale not only repeat the words over the lintel in the underground prison of the beautiful woman (which in their turn recall the lines written in gold above the door of the three ladies) but also are repeated by the magic words engraved on the horseman's lead tablet in the third tale. People are burned, whipped, tortured, and mutilated; lovers lose their loved ones; travelers lose their way; fantastic treasures are discovered and subsequently lost over and over again. In short, there seems to be no exclusive realm within which the action of each tale unfolds; instead, they share a common narrative universe. It is no wonder, then, that upon finishing the third dervish's tale, the reader wants to go back to the beginning, to start over again and try to sort it all out.

Part of the complication results from a multiplication of character in each tale which progresses incrementally as we move from one narrative to another. The first dervish, for example, is suggestively doubled by his cousin, with whom he has strong ties of affection, and this cousin in turn narcissistically extends himself by engaging in incestuous relations with his sister, an act that, particularly within the spatial boundaries imposed by the underground prison, limits the possibility of a confrontation between the self and anything that is not a part of the self. (It is worth remarking the punishment that attends this act within this narrative context.)

The duplication of character in the second dervish's story is, on one level at least, less troubling than the repeated mirroring of character in his predecessor's tale. Within the second narrative universe, one meets one's double, not in an actual physical encounter, but by being metamorphically transformed from one being to another. The second dervish never actually meets his double but rather assumes another self in his transformation from human to beast. The same holds true for the king's daughter and the evil jinn, who in the final series of metamorphoses repeatedly re-create themselves in a seemingly perpetual cycle of transformations that move beyond the restrictions of the larger animal realm to incorporate that of the vegetable and mineral as well. The self is duplicated, then, not by repeating itself but by becoming other, becoming different.

The third dervish's tale, appropriately, manipulates the multiplication of character in the most complicated fashion.

We are here once again back in a world of copies, of iconic repetitions; but this time it is not a question of doubling or tripling of character, as in the first dervish's tale, but rather of extensive and ever-increasing multiplication to the point of there being almost only sameness, repetition, without difference. This is clearly the case with the forty women of the magic castle, each of whom mirrors the other in an ever-repeating display of beauty. More interesting, however, is the third dervish's earlier encounter with, not one or two young men of similar aspect, but ten, all of whom are dressed in splendid clothes and blind in the right eye—a coincidence at which the dervish marvels: "I was approached by ten neatly dressed young men accompanied by an old man, and I was astonished to see that each young man was blind in the right eye, and marveled at this coincidence" (123–24).[21] What is important here is not only the multiplication of the same character but the fact that these youths prefigure what the third dervish and his comrades are themselves to become.

The corollary to this multiplication of character is a repetition of action, which can occur within the individual tales on two levels: either each of the multiplied characters repeats in his turn a specific act or, alternatively, a specific act is repeated time after time by the same character. Thus a significant—and sometimes insignificant—act is likely to occur repeatedly and often in close succession. The first dervish, in characteristically simple fashion, searches for the hidden tomb for at least four days in a row, an action that in its repetition almost leads to madness:

> Then I went to the graveyard and searched for the sepulcher, but I could not find it or remember anything about it. I kept wandering from sepulcher to sepulcher and from tomb to tomb, without stopping to eat or drink, until night set in. . . . Finally I went back to the house, ate a little, and spent a restless night. Having recollected everything he and I did that night, I returned the following

morning to the graveyard and wandered about, searching
till nightfall, without finding the sepulcher or figuring out
a way that might lead me to it. I went back to the graveyard
for a third day and a fourth and searched for the
sepulcher from early morning till nightfall without success, until I almost lost my sanity with frustration and
worry. (87–88)[22]

The second dervish, similarly, leaves the tailor's house
day after day for a year in order to go out into the forest to
chop wood:

Then [the tailor] bought me an axe and a rope and put me
under the charge of certain woodcutters. I went out with
them, cut wood all day long, and came back, carrying my
bundle on my head. I sold the wood for half a dinar and
brought the money to the tailor. In such work I spent an
entire year. (94–95)[23]

Only when the ritualistic pattern has been carefully established through repetition is it subsequently, and permanently, disturbed:

One day [after a year] I went out into the wilderness, and
having penetrated deep, I came to a thick patch of trees in
a meadow irrigated by running streams. When I entered
the patch, I found the stump of a tree, and when I dug
around it with my axe and shoveled the earth away, I came
upon a ring that was attached to a wooden plank. (95)[24]

It is the disturbance of this pattern of repeated daily action
that leads to the dervish's fateful encounter.

It is not until the third dervish's tale that the potential of
such repeated actions is fully explored, for here, for the first
time, the repetition of an act is shared by both subject and
predicate. Each of the slaves who attends the beautiful young
boy, for example, performs in unison with the others the
actions required by the establishment of the underground
hideaway. ("The black men kept going back and forth and

descending through the trap door with the articles until they had transported everything that was in the ship.") The dervish in his turn follows suit and once underground establishes a pattern of daily actions that he sustains for forty days, at which point he fulfills his predetermined fate. When he later encounters the ten blind men, he notes with surprise how each of them ritually blackens his face and beats his chest nightly for a month's time. And when, finally, the dervish insists upon learning the meaning of such bizarre and repeated actions, he arrives at the castle, where for exactly one full year he spends each night in the same way with one of the forty beautiful women and subsequently opens the forty magic doors. The moral of the tale, indeed of the cycle as a whole, seems to be that any act worth performing once is worth performing over and over again.

There is, finally, one larger act that recurs not only within the individual tales but throughout the cycle as a whole, an act that transcends mere action and is, in fact, one of the primary motivating forces behind the narrative. Violation, whether of law, custom, or simply request, lies at the heart of each of the dervishes' stories. Repeatedly they transgress, trespass, ignore limits, and defy injunctions they should rightfully obey. The first dervish helps—albeit unknowingly—his cousin to commit incest, to violate one of the primary laws of his society. The second dervish deliberately ignores the rules in the underground prison and conjures up the jinn. The third dervish repeatedly commits the most willful transgressions of all. Fully forewarned by his ten blind companions not to ask the reason for their nightly ritual, he persists in satisfying his intense curiosity; and despite the pleas of the forty beautiful women to obey their one request, he still opens the forbidden door. In each case, transgression results in the dervishes' misfortune. One would hope that by the time they arrive in Baghdad, they would have learned their lesson well; but history is destined to repeat itself. The three ladies state over and over again the ominous statute:

Speak not of what concerns you not, lest you hear what pleases you not. Yet at the first untoward occurrence, the dervishes throw caution to the wind and seek to know what should remain unknown.

Why this willful defiance of the lessons of experience? In part, certainly, because without such transgressive behavior, the dervishes would belie their disguise and the conditions of their newly acquired station as dervishes. But more important, because without such transgression, the dervishes would have no stories to tell and no cause to tell them. It is this drive to move beyond established limits and laws, to know the unknown and unusual, that gives the dervishes their stuff for narration. Todorov notes that it is the fixed law or established rule that immobilizes narrative, that stalls the necessary movement from an initial equilibrium to a final one. All narrative must partake of some transgressive deviance or disturbance if it is to progress from beginning to end. The fact that this transgressive movement is repeatedly thematized and thus foregrounded in the cycle of the porter and the three ladies, however, suggests its particular importance for this type of story in the *1001 Nights*. Without this impulse to transgress, not only would the dervishes be disturbing the necessary movement of narrative, but they could also tell only about life as we know and experience it; and the pleasure of such narratives, for the likes of kings and caliphs at least, would certainly be minimal. The porter and the shopper have no stories to tell because they have never moved beyond the boundaries of their native land. The three dervishes, as narrative-men, must repeatedly transgress, step beyond the preestablished limits, so that they will always have stories worth the telling.

III

The patterns of repetition I have dealt with thus far derive from the story level of the narrative and contribute largely to the organization of the cycle's structure. But equally prominent are the repetitions that occur on the level of discourse. True to its initiatory position, Burton's calligram establishes the visual model for such linguistic repetition and variation. Throughout the tales, the reader encounters the same phrases, the same sentences, the same patterns of language over and over again, often mirroring in miniature fashion their larger narrative counterparts.

Upon careful inspection, the text manifests a kind of linguistic repetition to which the Arabic language, largely because of its trilateral root system, is particularly given. The immediate connection between a verbal form and its nominal counterpart is not an unusual structure in Arabic prose, but its occurrence in the cycle of "The Porter and the Three Ladies" is especially frequent. The most common manifestation of this extension of a specific verbal root is the cognate accusative, the use of the accusative nominal form of a preceding verb to complete the action described by the verb. In the course of the thirty-eighth night alone, for example, this form occurs five times: "I wept a strong weeping,"[25] says the dervish when confronted with his executioner; and shortly thereafter he notes his uncle's identical response to his son's disappearance: "Then he wept a strong weeping."[26] The response is equally powerful when the uncle learns of his nephew's knowledge regarding his son's recent activities: "He rejoiced a strong rejoicing,"[27] and stated again with similar intensity when the dervish recognizes his cousin's underground hideaway: "I rejoiced a strong rejoicing."[28] The final action of this scene is, not surprisingly, equally pronounced. When the uncle realizes what his son has done, he "struck his son's face [with] a hard striking."[29] In each of these phrases, typical of the text as a whole, the noun nominally repeats the action of the verb for the general purpose of emphasis or intensification. In stories built upon actions or emotions of high intensity, it is not surprising that such constructions abound.

The cognate accusative does not, however, provide the only linguistic forum within which nouns and verbs derived from the same root repeat each other. One repeatedly encounters phrases or sentences that are built both nominally and verbally upon the same root. In most cases, such repetition implies either the completion or fulfillment of an initial action or the corresponding (and often mirroring) response. Thus in the above scene when the first dervish weeps before his executioner, he notes, "I wept bitterly over what had happened to me until I made him weep with me" (88),[30] using both the first form and the causative fourth form of the root BKY, "to weep." The second dervish, who is appropriately the master of such word games, provides another example. In describing the response of the ship captain to his metamorphosed self, he notes that the captain says, "Merchants, this ape is asking me for protection so I will protect him,"[31] a sentence that posits an initial request and its subsequent verbal fulfillment by relying on the tenth and the fourth forms of the root JWR, "to protect." Similarly, when the third dervish meets the young man in the underground cave, he notes, "Then I offered him something to eat, and after the two of us ate, I rose" (120),[32] a phrase that relies for its action on both the nominal and first verbal form of the verb AKL, "to eat," to indicate the dervish's instigation of an action and his subsequent participation in that action.

There are cases, however, in which linguistic repetition does not serve merely to extend or complement an initial action but rather to indicate with accuracy its actual repetition. In such cases, the locus of linguistic repetition is, in general, verbally limited. The second dervish, for example, remarks, "She took off my clothes and took off her clothes"[33] (in this example, the repetition extends to both predicate and object). Or in the case of the third dervish, we read: "When he fell asleep, I . . . slept" (119).[34] To some extent, of course, such repetition relies upon, or at least derives from, a certain multiplication of character. The reader is not surprised by, indeed anticipates, a similarity of movement or action when he or she encounters ten identical black slaves or ten young men all blind in the right eye.

Less expected is the repetition of an action by a single character; but as noted earlier, the cycle of the porter and the three ladies abounds in such repeated actions. As might be expected, the performative repetition of such actions is often linguistically underscored. In the previously cited description of the first dervish's search for his cousin's grave, for instance, he states:

> Then I went to the graveyard and searched for the sepulcher. . . . I kept wandering from sepulcher to sepulcher and from tomb to tomb, . . . until night set in. . . . I returned the following morning to the graveyard and wandered about, searching till nightfall. . . . I went back to the graveyard for a third day and a fourth and searched for the sepulcher from early morning till nightfall without success. (87–88)[35]

The action is established in all its compulsiveness through the repetition of key words such as tomb and sepulcher; while the extension of the action over time is indicated first through a summary of the action ("I returned the following morning to the graveyard and wandered about"), and subsequently by the adverbial marking of time's passing, "a third day and a fourth." This pattern recurs with variation throughout the cycle.[36] The third dervish notes with care the ritualistic behavior of his ten companions on the first night, indicates its repetition on the second night, remarks its repeated occurrence over a month's time, and finally summarizes the activity in its largest outlines—to make a long story short, as he says, recognizing implicitly the potential for boredom in such repeated actions. A similar narrative pattern supports the dervish's description of his nightly encounters with the forty beautiful women of the magic castle, though here an equally complete description of both the first and second encounters tempers the need for a final résumé of the general action. The dervish's final statement, "My lady, to make a long story short, for a full year I lived with them a carefree life," provides in conjunction with his previous description enough narrative scaffolding for the reader to make the necessary leap of imagination.

Perhaps the most significant of such linguistically patterned sequences in terms of both story and discourse is the third dervish's narration of his exploration of the ninety-nine magic rooms of the castle. The importance of this action has already been underscored by the ladies' commands regarding which of the rooms the dervish may enter. The dervish correspondingly details with care his entry into and discovery of the first several apartments:

> Then I went and opened the first chamber, and when I entered, I found myself in a garden with streams, trees, and abundant fruits. It was a garden like Paradise. . . . [A set piece and two poems describing the garden contained in this room follows.] At last I went out of the garden and closed the door.

> The following day I opened another door, and when I entered, I found myself in a large field full of palm trees and encircled by a running stream. . . . [A set piece describing a garden follows.] After I enjoyed and diverted myself there for a while, I went out and closed the door.

> Then I opened a third door and found myself in a large hall covered with all kinds of colored marble, rare metals, and precious stones. . . . There I enjoyed myself, felt happy, and forgot my cares.

> Then I went to sleep, and in the morning I opened a fourth door and found myself in a large hall, surrounded by forty chambers whose doors stood open. I entered every chamber and found them full of jewels, such as pearls, emeralds, rubies, corals, and carbuncles, as well as gold and silver. . . . 'O my lady, I enjoyed myself in chamber

after chamber until thirty-nine days had passed and there remained only one day and one night. During that time, I had opened all ninety-nine chambers, and there remained only the hundredth, the one the girls had cautioned me not to open.

. . . I was no longer able to restrain myself and succumbing to the devil, at last opened the door plated with gold. As soon as I entered, I was met by a perfume. . . . (129–31)[37]

Clearly, a patterned set of actions supported by an equally patterned, indeed almost formulaic, mode of discourse has been established. As always, repetition is attended by difference. Although the dervish repeatedly opens a door, enters a room, and discovers an open space that he then describes in set-piece fashion, he does not always leave it in the same manner. On the third night, in fact, the act of departure is replaced, narratively speaking at least, by somnolence; while the end of the fourth night slips from narrative sight altogether. As if to compensate for such gaps, however, the dervish's final fully described foray into the permitted ninety-nine rooms includes a box-within-a-box discovery of forty open doors that lead to even greater wonders. The function of such a spatially framed miniature of the episode's larger structure seems clear. Not only does it recall to the reader the larger dimensions of the sequence, but in conjunction with the patterned movement and discourse, it also eases the reader into the condensation of time and action suggested in the dervish's subsequent summary of his activity. It is only with the significant opening of the final forbidden door that the dervish returns to a more expanded discourse. Even at this important juncture, however, he resorts to the motions and corresponding discourse we have come to expect.

One can easily slip at this point from an examination of linguistic repetition within the context of repeated action to

an examination of words and phrases whose repetition occurs solely on the level of discourse. The distinction is a
difficult one to maintain, for the discourse value of a statement can never be totally divorced from its story value.
There are, however, cases where a statement or statements
are repeated, not to indicate the repetition of an action, but
rather to indicate the recurrence of a more or less static
narrative condition of the text, generally in the way of situation, context, or commentary. The frame story provides the
richest examples of such linguistic repetition, since it is that
part of the story responsible for establishing the larger context for the ensuing narrative action. The injunction of the
three women, for example—Speak not of what concerns you
not, lest you hear what pleases you not—is repeated no less
than six times with slight variation in the course of the frame
story, thereby establishing one of the primary laws of this
particular narrative universe.[38] To somewhat different effect
is the implicit triple repetition of the proverbial statement "If
[my story] were engraved with needles at the corner of the
eye, [it] would be a warning to those who wish to consider"
(85),[39] a statement made directly by the first dervish and
then narratively resumed and repeated by the storyteller,
who says simply, "Then she [the lady] questioned the second
dervish, and he said the same, and questioned the third, and
again he replied like the other two." (Interestingly, the same
proverb is repeated by the first lady at the start of her story.)
The point here is not so much to attest to the exemplary
nature of the tales, since that aspect has already been implicitly belied by the storyteller's repeated errors; but rather
to indicate their narrative aspect, to highlight their nature as
narratives, indeed as remarkable narratives.

Perhaps the most obvious and yet least intrusive of such
repeated statements is the abrupt third-person interruption
that occurs at the end of each night. At the close of each
night the reader encounters some variation on the statement, "And morning overtook Shahrazad and she lapsed

into silence." This is followed by the identification of the number of the next night, for example, "The sixty-third night," spatially set off from the rest of the text, and the explicit continuation of Shahrazad's narrative, for example, "The following night Shahrazad said, I heard, O happy King, that . . . ," at which point Shahrazad's narrative voice gives way to that of the person telling the story. So often and regularly does this interruption occur that by the time we have reached, say, the fifteenth night, we no longer take conscious note of the literal meaning of the night break but simply acknowledge it for what it is—a narrative device for marking and, as we shall see, ultimately distorting the linear movement of time. Once again, the narrative aspect of the work, this time in temporal guise, is underscored.

There is one final mode of linguistic repetition that, although not unrelated to those already discussed, deviates in its specific locus of repetition. In the above discussion of the statement "Speak not of what concerns you not, lest you hear what pleases you not," I remarked that in a specific context, a statement could be repeated at various points in the narrative. There is, though, an additional level at which repetition within this and similar statements occurs, a level concerned not so much with the actual words of the statement as with the patterns created by the interrelations among its component parts. The above-quoted injunction is written in *saj'*, rhymed prose, a style often reserved for works whose verbal texture is to be brought to the fore. The statement accordingly adheres to a parallel if somewhat loose rhythmic and rhyming scheme:

> lā tatakallamū fī-mā lā ya'nīkum
> tasma'ū mā lā yurḍīkum.

The injunction is built upon an obvious syntactical, semantic, and rhythmic parallelism. The two verbs that anchor the statement, *tatakallamū* and *tasma'ū,* function reciprocally in semantic terms by juxtaposing the related activities of speaking and hearing; and although they do not follow the same verbal paradigm, they both repeat the same initial and final sounds. A similar relation obtains between the two dependent verbs of the statement, *ya'nīkum* and *yurḍīkum*. Here both verbs conform to the third-person singular paradigm of the tertia weak root ending in *ya*. In this case, though, the verbal parallels are extended not semantically but by the addition of the pronominal suffix *-kum* to both verbs. Again, rhythmic parallels are intensified by aural ones. Finally, the parallels are rounded out by the equal distribution of the pronoun *mā* following the two main verbs (although the first is followed by the preposition *fī*), and the repeated, though this time syntactically transposed, negative particle *lā*. In sum, the statement is built solely upon a sequence of parallel and repeating sounds and rhythms.

Instances of rhymed prose occur throughout the cycle of "The Porter and the Three Ladies," and they are not limited to the repeated statements of the ladies' injunctions. As often as not, extended descriptions in the *1001 Nights* are stylistically based upon *saj'*. Thus, for example, the narrator's description of the first woman or the third dervish's description of the first magic room. But the incidence of poetry in this cycle is quite high as well and generally occurs for purposes of emphasis or elaboration, often in conjunction with these extended descriptions. When the first dervish wants to win the sympathy of his executioner, he recites a poem aimed at enlisting his aid—a rhetorical flourish to which the executioner himself poetically responds; similarly, when the beautiful lady of the underground chamber wants to underscore her pleasure at the visit of the second dervish, she poetically details the preparations she would have made had she known of his coming. The third dervish's narrative does not ignore such poetic emphases. When the dervish and the old man want to express their profound sadness at the death of the young boy, they both indulge in prolonged poetic

lamentations; and, in a different key, when the dervish wants
to supplement his descriptions of the wondrously beautiful
women and splendid rooms (often initially presented in
rhymed prose), he unreservedly plunges into poetic recita-
tion in which he reiterates their various qualities and characteristics.

The kind of repetition that occurs in such instances can
exist on several levels. The third dervish's description of the
beautiful woman with whom he spends his first night in the
magic castle provides a representative example of the way in
which such poetic discourse functions. The dervish initially
describes the woman in prose, though, significantly, even
this brief description lapses quickly into *saj'*. Already, then,
the above-mentioned parallelisms and repetitions initiated
by rhymed prose are established. Even this elaborate form of
prose composition, however, is incapable of containing, of
fully expressing, the dervish's response to the woman's
beauty. He naturally takes refuge in the words of the poet to
supplement his description. Semantically, this poem repeats
the preceding prose description, which in its turn has provided a locus for a kind of formal repetition. In the first four
lines of the poem the narrator reiterates poetically the various aspects of the woman's beauty. Formally, of course, the
verses provide the much stricter parallelisms and repetitions
of poetry. Not only is the metrical scheme maintained
throughout the poem, but it is supplemented by both the
strict monorhyme that vertically connects each verse to the
next and the less strict and more occasional rhyme at the end
of each hemistich, which provides a connection between one
hemistich and both its horizontal and vertical coordinates. In
addition, the linguistic repetitions and variations that often
attend such poetry are here in evidence. Both hemistiches of
the fifth verse are built upon the fifth form of the verb
ShBH, "to compare"; similarly, the second hemistich of the
sixth verse plays upon the nominal *mashrab,* "drink," in both
its nominative and accusative forms. Such linguistic play is

maintained in a somewhat altered fashion in the seventh and eighth verses. Instead of strict verbal repetition, however, variational play on a particular root is introduced. *Al-qawātil*, "the killers," of the first hemistich of the third line becomes *al-qatīl*, "the killed one," of the second hemistich; and similarly, the verbal action of desiring expressed in *ṣabawtu* is extended and intensified in its cognate accusative *ṣabwatan*. Linguistic, formal, and semantic repetitions abound. It is yet another indication that the repetitive mode has taken hold.

IV

It should be clear by now that the repetitive mode has indeed been dominant through to the close of the third dervish's tale. From the opening of the frame story, when the porter meets the shopper in the market and is instructed to carry her packages, we are, in fact, already within the grasp of the repetitive,[40] a narrative mode that, as discussed above, achieves its summa in the tales of the three dervishes. To analyze the subsequent stories of the two ladies within this context would be superfluous and redundant. It would also, undeniably, be less fruitful. Each of the tale-telling women is one of three sisters, just as each of the dervishes is one of three companions-in-misfortune; the sisters of the eldest woman repeat the same actions with the same consequences; the young prince whom she meets in the petrified city tells of the repeated calls urging his people to follow Islam; and the story makes some use of the above-noted patterns of linguistic repetition. But it is more difficult to locate such repetitions within the second lady's tale, which maintains a rather singular narrative line; and the shopper, of course, ultimately has no tale to tell, thereby disturbing the initial grouping of the three women established in the frame story.

What has occurred during the course of the two women's stories is a gradual attenuation of the symmetrical and therefore repetitive structures upon which the cycle has been premised. To deny the dominance of such structures because of this subsequent attenuation would be to ignore the undeniable significance and prominence of repetition as a mode of narrative discourse in general and within this cycle especially. One must, instead, finally question what function the repetitive mode serves; why the three ladies, who seem to inaugurate a kind of discourse premised upon repetition, are the very ones who are ultimately least susceptible to its narrative manipulation; why elements connected through relations of repetition rather than those connected through relations of contiguity dominate the larger pattern of this cycle; and why this structure at the last gives way to the more conventional linear pattern of narrative construction. In the light of these questions, the final dissolution of the repetitive structure provides a kind of control, offers through its difference a confirmation of the fundamental value and function of the various kinds of narrative repetition found in this work.

Chapter Five

Magic Time
The Movement and Meaning of Narrative Repetition

> But he who does not comprehend that life is a repetition
> and that this is the beauty of life, has condemned himself
> and deserves nothing better than what is sure to befall
> him, namely, to perish.
>
> —Søren Kierkegaard, *Repetition*

I

WE come finally to the crucial connection between repetition and time, a connection that, although of particular interest vis-à-vis the repetitive mode, is of course maintained with all types of narrative discourse. For all narrative must take first root in the temporal realm. Indeed, not only must narrative move within the various confines of its own temporal boundaries, but we as readers can participate in narrative only by following the temporal continuum of our own universe, by establishing a time of reading. What is the relation between these two temporal spheres? How does one clock narrative time so that the reader's sense of time remains

mains intact? How can one move forward or backward in narrative time without destroying the limits of temporality? The answers differ according to individual narrative genre and effect. Epic, romance, realist novel: each genre requires a different temporal perspective specific to its narrative structure. But regardless of generic constraints, each must engage on some level with Proust's "jeu formidable . . . avec le Temps."

In the cycle of "The Porter and the Three Ladies," it is primarily the repeated recurrence of certain patterned structures of story and discourse which undeniably and somewhat ironically signals the movement of the cycle in time and the correlative unfolding of the narrative. One must again remember that exact identity between repeated events of whatever nature is, strictly speaking, impossible; that the linear constraints of the temporal realm must necessarily prevent the exact repetition of events no matter how similar, simply because any repeated event occurs at a time later than that of the instigating event. At best, narrative can know only near repetition, the replaying of the same events, the same verbal components at a different time.[1] The very fact that the same phrase exists at one or more points in a text points to the necessary temporal movement of the narrative, its incapacity to maintain a static position. In the third dervish's description of the opening of the forbidden doors, for example, the repetition of both story and discourse underscores not only the significance of the act of discovery but both the temporal movement that accompanies the act and the narrative that describes it. The repeated interruption at the end of each night serves much the same function—only in this case the act being described is that of narration itself. In short, given the insistent foregrounding of repetition as a means of structuring narrative discourse, the *1001 Nights* seems to be telling us something significant about the relation between time, repetition, and narrative.

That repetition within narrative is essentially a temporal

phenomenon cannot be disputed, since without the context of advancing linear time, repetition has no frame of reference and therefore no meaning. A narrative structured by repetition consequently relies upon and often silently points to its temporal framework. Not surprisingly, then, time is of the essence, both structurally and thematically, in the three ladies cycle. Everyone is trying to beat the clock in both narrative and performative terms, and time's passage accordingly assumes critical importance. Repetition appropriately underscores this temporal movement.

I will return to this crucial relationship shortly, but let me digress briefly here to note that other levels of narrative time are operative within the cycle as a whole. While the repetition of structures of story and discourse is sustained primarily on the horizontal plot axis of the narrative and accordingly manipulates the temporal movement within the individual narratives, there is a corresponding vertical axis along which the temporal movement of the act of narration itself moves. This temporal movement can be designated as narrational time, that time specific to a given act of narration. Given the basic repetition of the narrative act within the cycle, as discussed earlier, the corresponding temporal movement is clearly significant.

We must again go back to the beginning. The first level of time specific to the narrative act—and there is here an equivalence between narrative time and narrative voice—is that in which the storyteller tells his story about Shahrazad telling her stories. This level of primary narration remains largely implicit and substantially unvoiced. It is, in fact, brought to the fore only in the interruption that occurs at the end of each night—"But morning overtook Shahrazad, and she lapsed into silence"—and in the occasional voice markers, "said Shahrazad," which necessarily follow this interruption. The second level of narrational time and voice is appropriately that of Shahrazad herself. This level is only slightly more pronounced than that of the primary narrator; indeed, since both share the third-person past tense, it is easy to mistake the one for the other. The only time Shahrazad's voice comes through clearly is at the beginning of each night when she refers to herself in the first person and directly addresses the king: "I heard, O happy King." But it should be emphasized that within the primary narrative of the story-teller, the time and voice of Shahrazad are themselves primary; they repeat the function of the time and voice within which they are embedded. It is within their limits that the most substantial narratives of the cycle unfold.

The Chinese box syndrome continues. The third level of narrational time belongs to the story being told by Shahrazad. This is the realm which is initially indicated by the indeterminate equivalent of the implicit "once upon a time" that opens the three ladies cycle, but which is later specified by Shahrazad as the time of Harun al-Rashid. It is in this time that the characters of the tale exist and tell their own stories. In the case of the three ladies cycle, this level is established initially in the frame story and subsequently reasserted in the intervals that separate the individual tales. It is at this point that the story is evaluated and its narrator summarily dismissed. At the end of the first tale, for example, the dervish concludes: "But God drove us to your house, and you were kind and generous enough to let us in and help me forget the loss of my eye and the shaving off of my beard"; and the narrative continues: "The girl said to him, 'Stroke your head and go.' He replied, 'By God, I will not go until I hear the tales of the others.' . . . It is related, O happy King, that those who were present marveled at the tale of the first dervish. The caliph said to Ja'far, 'In all my life I have never heard a stranger tale.' Then the second dervish came forward and said: . . ." (91–92).[2] Again, the third-person past tense prevails. The voice is ostensibly Shahrazad's, but the tone of the narrative bears a strong resemblance to that of an unspecified, omniscient narrator. It would seem that the further back in narrational time we go, the fainter the original narrative voice becomes.

The loss of the primary narrative voice—be it that of the storyteller or of Shahrazad—is finalized in the fourth level of narrational time. This is that time in which the narrative-men and -women speak, a time that is necessarily antecedent to that of the act of narration. These stories are also told in the past tense, but there is here a switch in the narrative voice from the third person to the first person: "Then the first dervish came forward and said: 'My lady, the cause of *my* eye being torn out and *my* beard being shaved off was as follows. *My* father was a king . . .'" (emphasis added) (86).[3] A complete narrative transition involving the transference of the authoritative narrative voice and a corresponding shift in the level of narrational time has been made.

With the exception of the narrative night markers, nowhere else in the cycle is the passing of time noted with such care as it is in this final narrational realm. Each dervish makes a deliberate point of marking the amount of time spent in any given place. The first dervish spends four days looking for his cousin. The second dervish spends one year chopping wood. The beautiful woman has spent twenty-five years in her underground prison; the demon comes to stay with her once every ten days; and she rather calculatingly informs her new-found companion: "He has been away for four days, so there remain only six days before he comes again. Would you like to spend five days with me and leave on the day before he arrives?" (96).[4] The third dervish in his turn sails at sea for forty days before the storm; he spends forty days with the boy whom he eventually kills, and one year minus forty days with the women in the palace. Clearly, time's passage has a peculiar significance within these tales, as if the careful marking of time were to compensate for the narrative and corresponding temporal distance that has been traveled between the primary narrative and those at the furthest narrational remove. Yet no matter how deep into the past we travel with the dervishes, and no matter how long they stay there, we and they all end up in the same place in and at the same time. In the end, we all rejoin the narrative present.

What results is a fundamental disturbance and confusion of temporal levels within the work as a whole and the cycle in particular. In addition to the standard horizontal range of the temporal spectrum within which narrative can move from left to right at ease, the three ladies cycle offers as well vertical levels of time whose only connection is that the one contains the other. If within each level a certain horizontal progression (or regression as is often the case) occurs, it is eventually confounded by the narrative constraints restricting each level. In short, a simple diachronic, linear connection in time cannot be made among the individual tales within the cycle. As the story unfolds, one must move up and down within the various levels of narrational time as well as back and forth in narrative time. A fundamental jarring of temporal perspective occurs.

Ultimately, one of the main reasons it is so difficult to maintain a distinction among the separate stories of the cycle, to remember what the *1001 Nights* narrative of "The Porter and the Three Ladies" is all about—a difficulty I suspect every reader encounters—is because the line against which the narrative unfolds is so deviant. It is a difficulty that the use of repetition as a mode of narrative discourse largely maintains and essentially instigates; indeed, the vertical movement of narrational times and voices is itself little more than the echoing, the verbal mirroring of one time and voice by another. That narrative repetition has no significance without a linear temporal base, indeed derives its essence from its temporal affiliation, is clear. What is not so clear, perhaps, is that by its very nature repetition is an attempt to destroy its own essence, to kill the natural movement of linear time, to turn time back upon itself, to make time repeat itself, reflect itself, do anything but continue its unimpeded advance. That such an attempt is ultimately fruitless is the necessary result of the condition that all narrative must somehow move from one point to another, from beginning to end by way of the middle, if it is to maintain its status not only as narrative but as a linguistic construct. The fact remains, however, that every effort has been made to slow this movement, indeed to subvert this movement, to alter the inevitable march of narrative time without altering the fundamental nature of narrative.

One of the prerogatives of any narrative is to play with time, to create its own time. If the *1001 Nights* is a narrative telling about the making and telling of other narratives, it is also necessarily a work about the relation between narratives, or specific types of narrative, and their temporal foundation. The motivating force behind Shahrazad's telling of the *1001 Nights* is, as it is for her counterparts in Baghdad, a desire to forestall death, to impede time's natural flow, to ward off the sense of an ending. At the behest of their audience, these tellers of tales must kill time, or be killed themselves. It is ironic but essential that in order to kill time, and thereby to avoid the inevitable end of time, the narrators must make time, create narrative time. Not surprisingly, they narratively manifest this irony by developing their tales according to repetitive structures of story and discourse which counteract the forward movement of time and in so doing undercut the fundamental impulse of narrative.

II

It stands to reason that this effort to forestall the inevitable human end of time, the physical sense of an ending, affects the narrative sense of an ending as well. Given that narrative repetition is essentially a kind of recurrent textual return, a backward narrative movement that seeks to reunite, realign a later textual moment with its original preceding one, it is not surprising that the ending of a work structured according to various patterns of repetition is significantly different from that of a work that progresses more or less straightforwardly from beginning to end. Peter Brooks notes that in the grammar of plot, "repetition, taking us back again over the same ground, could have to do with the choice of ends."[5] The pertinent suggestion is that the ending of a repetitive narrative functions differently in relation to the preceding whole. The particular intent of this difference is focused on the narrative beginning.

If one accepts Todorov's premise that the ideal narrative consists in its broadest outlines of a fundamentally stable situation (the beginning), which is subsequently disturbed (the middle), and finally resolved (the end)—that is, that any narrative moves between two equilibriums that are related but not identical (the same but different)—one looks to the ending of a traditional narrative as a resolution marked by its necessarily later difference from the beginning.[6] In short, the movement inherent in any narrative structure requires a distance between beginning and end along which the narrative can unfold, and this distance in turn requires a difference between the two limiting points of the narrative. The absence of this distance of difference would seemingly lead to a kind of narrative collapse, an inability on the part of narrative to pursue its necessary course. A repetitive narrative, however, a narrative whose structural impulse is always to look backward, to turn back upon itself, necessarily subverts this sense of an ending as something in the distant and different future.

The cycle of "The Porter and the Three Ladies" drives the point home. When the second woman has finished her tale and the caliph has ordered that it be entered as a recorded history and placed in the treasury, the closing frame of the story as told by Shahrazad to the king follows. This last section of the tale, structurally separated from the preceding section of the narrative by a night break, fulfills much the same function as an epilogue. Not only are the primary characters of all five embedded tales gathered together at one time and in one place, but the future of each one is irrevocably determined by the political and narrative authorities in question, with some assistance from a dea ex machina in the guise of a Muslim ifrit. In sum, the ultimate conclusion of the narrative, the final weaving together of assorted narrative strands, is achieved.

What happens at the end of the three ladies cycle is not unlike what happens at the happy end of a nineteenth-century novel: people are married; losses are compensated; futures are ensured. The ifrit is instrumental in this activity. In gestures that remind us that at a certain point it is potentially the women in this tale who wield the power (especially the narrative power), she helps to bring the cycle to its close by releasing the two sisters of the eldest lady from their inhuman captivity as black bitches and by informing the caliph of the true identity of the second woman's jealous husband, who, conveniently, is both geographically and genetically close at hand. Harun al-Rashid then takes over and asserts his secular authority. He expediently marries the three sisters of the first woman's story to the three dervishes, whom he subsequently enlists as his chamberlains; he reunites the second woman with his son, her estranged husband; and he obligingly offers himself as a spouse to the third woman, the shopper, who curiously is richly rewarded for having no story to tell. A fearful, perhaps because unearthly, symmetry results. It is no wonder that at the close of the entire narrative, the caliph orders that all the preceding stories be recorded and thereby preserved for posterity.

What has happened at the end of this cycle is remarkable for reasons other than its patterned design. Instead of progressing toward a future state, a condition distantly different because later than the beginning, the narrative has moved backward, has restored its characters to a time and a state predating that of the cycle's opening. The narrative has been markedly conservative, even retrograde in its driving impulse. When the ifrit, muttering words that no one can understand, releases the two women from bestial captivity, she expresses in summary form the basic thrust of the cycle's ending. The women return to their original state; the three dervishes reacquire their royal status (the narrative interestingly reminds us of this, as if to underline the socially conservative nature of the caliph's act: "He married the first girl and her sisters who had been cast under a spell to the three dervishes, who were the sons of kings" [150]).[7] And finally, the doorkeeper is returned to her former husband. The happy end of the cycle has not provided a new and different because importantly later equilibrium on which the narrative can rest. It has, on the contrary, done little more than return the narrative to an earlier state, one prior to that of its beginning. The status quo has been reestablished. Time has not doggedly marched onward and taken its inevitable toll; it has, in fact, moved backward and ultimately been frozen through narrative at a still and stable moment.

III

I would like now to move from this discussion about the conservative power of repetition to examine the way in which this narrative pattern relates to issues centering on the female body and questions of gender raised earlier in this study. Such generic issues of narrative time are not, I would suggest, unrelated to the way that gender (the etymological connection between genre and gender is here significant) means in a given narrative context. And they are particularly connected to the kinds of power struggles that gender, almost by definition, elicits.

Such struggles are at the very center of *Alf Laylah*. Indeed, one might argue that the text itself is instigated by the unanticipated appropriation of power by women. It is worth digressing to reexamine the familiar though crucial first scene. Shahzaman, Shahrayar's brother, has returned to his palace to find his wife in bed with a cook. Shahzaman responds to this scene by cutting his wife and her lover in two, only to discover some time later his brother's wife in a similar situation. This time, however, the treachery is magnified. Twenty concubines initially accompany the queen into the garden, ten of whom quickly reveal themselves to be men, specifically black slaves. Shahrayar's wife then allies herself with another black slave, who descends from a tree in response to her call. The scene is repeated a second time for the voyeuristic and legalistic benefit of Shahrayar, following which the two brothers go forth to seek comfort in the possibility of similar wrongdoing.

In an article entitled "Infidelity and Fiction," Judith Grossman has examined this scene with an eye to the question of women's subjectivity in the *1001 Nights* and has argued that what Shahzaman and Shahrayar are encountering here is "the problem which the recognition of female subjectivity has set for male-dominated cultures";[8] that the two brothers are confronting the fact that women have autonomous desires and, perhaps more frightening, the capacity to satisfy these desires at the expense of the "normal" boundaries of patriarchal society and culture. What is particularly interesting, though, is that it is not simply the women in whom these subversive desires are embodied. Shahzaman's wife, one recalls, was found with a cook, a representative of the domestic realm; while Shahrayar's wife, whose garden party suggests the way such subversive gestures are fruitful and multiply, has her male cohorts assume female guise, further intensifying this association between the feminine and the subversive. That her lover is himself black and a marginal figure (suggested by his tree-house location) suggests that such subversive behavior is distributed among all those who are not part of the dominant hierarchy. Clearly, speaking about gender is a constant reminder of the other categories of difference, such as race and class, that structure culture.

The response of the two kings to the potential for social revolution within their realm is to eradicate the threat in an effort to maintain the status quo. Both destroy the actual bodies that have sinned against authority, though it is interesting that while Shahzaman wreaks his own vengeance, Shahrayar delegates the punitive action to his wazir, Shahrazad's father, perhaps thereby formally asserting his unqualified resumption of power. Since it is precisely the declaration of unrestrained sexuality and desire that inaugurates this potential revolution, it makes perfect sense within the logic of the situation to mutilate the body that is the locus of such threatening actions.

It is not for nothing, I would argue, that as the interlude in "The Porter and the Three Ladies" has suggested, the *1001 Nights* is haunted by bodies. Bodies scarred, transported, naked, metamorphosed, bodies that seem incapable of maintaining a secure, stable, respectable position in society are, in a sense, the signature of *Alf Laylah*.[9] There are three groups of these specifically female bodies both in the frame tale and again in "The Porter and the Three Ladies of Baghdad" that are worth examining in order to explore the ways in which sex and text, male and female, come to grips with each other in this work, and to suggest thereby one kind of power struggle generated both in and by the *Nights* as well as the way the narrative, as suggested above, resolves it.

As Grossman notes, the presence that immediately counters the precipitating actions of those first female bodies, those of the kings' wives, is, surprisingly, not Shahrazad, but the woman possessed by the demon. Having discovered the betrayal of Shahrayar's wife, Shahzaman and his brother have responded by going forth to compare their fate with that of other men. Soon after their departure from the city they encounter a woman whose body, if not spirit, is quite literally possessed by a demon who contains her in a glass box with four padlocks. (The fact that the chest is glass is interesting because it gives the illusion of free will and movement.) It is this woman who forces the two brothers to have intercourse with her, as she has done with many hundreds of men before them, and it is, consequently, this woman who convinces them of the essential depravity and subversive nature of the feminine. It is after encountering her that Shahrayar returns home and implements his plan of daily execution. Grossman remarks that what is particularly noteworthy here is that the authority commanded by the woman is not her own. In clear bondage to her demon husband, she is only able to manipulate her situation within the terms of power established by the one who possesses her body. She can only compel Shahzaman and Shahrayar to do her bidding by invoking the power of her husband. Three times she threatens the two brothers with the wrath and ensuing violence of the ifrit if they deny her satisfaction; and although she brings her encounter with Shahzaman and Shahrayar to a close by pronouncing, "When a woman desires something, no one can stop her" (10),[10] what neither she nor the kings realize is that she is doing so according to the conditions established by a society that legislates the possession of the female body. She is not acting subversively; she is simply appropriating the power that belongs to her husband.

The woman who is eventually summoned by this encounter is Shahrazad. But I would like to return for the moment to those three Baghdadian women, who mirror not only Shahrazad in their commanding narrative presence and power but also—in their ultimate narrative objectification and confinement—those women she sets out to redeem. I argued earlier in this study that what the three ladies are doing in the frame story of their cycle is establishing a specific kind of discourse, a discourse that focuses on the female body and on the relation of this body to metaphoric language. These are, apparently, the first fully self-possessed, seemingly integral and unmarked female bodies that the reader encounters in the *Nights* (though this cycle is immediately followed by "The Story of the Three Apples," a story ostentatiously generated by the discovery of a mutilated female body). These are women who, apparently, not only control their own bodies and celebrate their own sexuality but also determine their own language and their own narrative rules. When the women demand further on in the frame tale that the men who have joined them for the evening either tell their tales or be permanently silenced, they are asserting their prerogative as the essential lawmakers in this particular realm.

It would seem that these three women are establishing an alternative society with radically different customs and laws that they themselves have determined. The specifically feminine space that they inhabit and that separates them from medieval Baghdad, the autonomous control they have over their own bodies, their legislative powers, which are backed by both oral and written authority and unquestioningly asserted, all suggest that within the confines of the frame tale at least, the actions and aims of these women are driven by anything but a desire to maintain the status quo of the society from which they have divorced themselves.

Indeed it seems that the three ladies are anxious to throw into question the values of those men who enter their privileged realm. But the facts of the extended narrative tell otherwise. The women's power turns out to be short-lived and confined to the initiating frame. It takes only the simple assertion of the real, historical, and political power of Harun al-Rashid, the embodiment of the dominant, established culture, to override the women's voices. Ja'far states: "You are in the presence of the seventh of the sons of 'Abbas, al-Rashid, son of al-Mahdi son of al-Hadi and brother of al-Saffah son of Mansur. Take courage, be frank, and tell the truth and nothing but the truth, and do not lie, for 'you should be truthful even if truth sends you to burning Hell'" (134).[11] And once commanded by this authority, the three ladies re-voke the essential rule of their realm, Speak not of what concerns you not, lest you hear what pleases you not, and obey the caliph's commands that they tell their own story—the truth and nothing but the truth.

The result of this all-too-ready abdication of power on the part of the three women leads to the reestablishment, or, since it has never really been threatened, the reassertion, of historical authority and the status quo it embodies. Again, the closing frame of the cycle as told by Shahrazad to Shahrayar drives the point home. The potential for a state of change and difference, a state in which the linguistic and social order suggested by the three ladies might be enacted, has been abolished. The interlude initiated by the three ladies has proved to be just that—a playful, insignificant moment prior to real action whose suggestions for rewriting the social and linguistic codes have been appropriated by the proper authorities. In this light it seems important to note that the bodies these three women so proudly reveal in the opening frame are not as whole and unmarked as they ini-tially appear. The back of the doorkeeper bears the tell-tale traces of a previous whipping, and it is these signs that ini-tially excite the caliph's curiosity. Significantly, the caliph himself, by association, is responsible for these bodily etch-ings since, ironically, it is his son who has engraved them on the woman's back.

There is one more encounter with a dis-rupted body in this cycle that warrants examination. Physical metamorphosis—the transformation of a person from one bodily state to another—occurs almost as frequently in the *Nights* as physi-cal mutilation. Both men and women are subject to meta-morphic transformation, though women seem more likely to lose their human aspect than men. The great example of metamorphosis in the three ladies cycle is, of course, that of the king's daughter, who through her powers of auto-metamorphosis releases the second dervish from bestial captivity.

The incident is interesting in part because of the way it plays off of earlier moments of physical enclosure or transformation. The dervish whom the princess redeems has been transformed as a result of his encounter with the woman in the underground cave. This woman, held there against her will by an ifrit, is, in essence, a duplicate of that other woman in captivity, discussed earlier, who instigates Shahrayar's revenge. The underground woman is content to entertain her unexpected, and indeed uninvited, visitor until she needs to fulfill her obligations to the ifrit in much the same way that her double economically uses the short measure of the demon's sleep to assert her own desires. Their fates, however, are radically different. The demon husband responds to the woman's infraction of justice by engaging in nothing less than physical torture and mutilation. (The dervish reports first, "Then he [the demon] seized her, stripped her naked and, binding her hands and feet to four stakes, proceeded to torture her"; and later, "I saw the girl stripped naked, her limbs tied, and her sides bleeding"; and finally, "Then he took the sword and struck the girl, severing her arm from her shoulder and sending it flying. Then he struck again and severed the other arm and sent it flying" (98–101).[12]

For his part in the deception, the dervish is transformed into an ape, but an ape who, critically, can still write though not speak. In order to release him, the king's daughter herself willingly undergoes a series of stunning metamorphoses during which she engages in combat with the ifrit, who counters with his own transformations. What is unusual about this encounter is that the princess alone controls what happens to her body. Her intellectual and corresponding metamorphic powers have been transmitted to her by an old woman (emphasizing, perhaps, the connection between such powers and the feminine) and are unbeknownst even to her father, who values her over a hundred sons. In her capacity for autonomy and self-determination, she counters the previous images of contained and possessed women with the image of a female body so supple and unbounded that it can change shape at will. Indeed, in her metamorphic powers, she recalls the three ladies and their metaphoric powers—both united in their potential to alter the given structure of reality. The affiliation, unfortunately, extends further, for like these other women, the princess's power is only temporary and, indeed, self-destructive. In working to release the second dervish from his bestial form, the princess effects not only the death of the ifrit but her own annihilation as well. Her final transformation into a heap of ashes suggests the ultimate ineffectualness of her power. In order to reestablish the "natural" order of things, in order to reassert the "normal" boundaries that structure society—the division between human and animal, between higher and lower, between male and female—the princess must extinguish her own "unnatural" powers precisely because they threaten such order. It is striking in this context that the dervish, who is both the instigator of all this trouble and one of the primary beholders of this scene, escapes almost wholly intact. The lost eye, the only mark he bears of this encounter, is the price he must pay for having borne witness, for having seen what should not be seen or even allowed to become visible. What the king's daughter has done is to stave off the breakdown of all "normal," established boundaries and limits, a breakdown that would force a reorganization of reality in the same way that the metaphoric language of the three ladies would. In sum, what she has indicated through her metamorphosis and consequent death, and what the three ladies themselves ultimately acknowledge, is the necessity, perhaps even the desirability, of returning society to its earlier patriarchal state.

IV

I would argue that the use of repetition in this narrative is the structural device that has worked its will in this re-establishment, in this conservative movement back to an earlier, more stable moment before narrative became necessary. For the most part, in any case. But what of the stories of the two women, which bring the embedded portion of the cycle to an asymmetric close? Why the growing attenuation of repetitive patterns of story and discourse precisely at that point closest to the final return, the final inversion of beginning and end, achieved by the frame's close? The answer lies in the very nature of the narrative movement associated with repetitive structures. If, as discussed earlier, such a narrative does move in a fashion contrary to that of a more horizontal, linear narrative; if repetition as a mode of narrative discourse structurally urges a narrative to return to its origins, ever to antecede its narrative beginnings, the narrative must, in practical storytelling terms, never end, for it must always and eternally repeat itself at the very point of its real narrative beginning. No matter how hard a narrative might try to counteract the sense of an ending as a future moment, then, it must inevitably concede at some point to the basic dictates of the narrative movement it is subverting. A practical end point must be located, since the potential of and for repetition is infinite. The endlessly repeating is, in fact, the interminable; there is theoretically no way to halt a narrative that has embarked on a fundamentally repetitive course. Just as metaphor must have metonymy in order to achieve its final metaphoric state, so must a repetitive narrative engage in a forward movement not only to assert the very fact of its repetition but also to bring the narrative at some arbitrary point to its practical close.

I would suggest that the final two tales of this cycle gradually provide a counter to this overriding movement of repetition; that in unwinding the ever more complicated structures of the preceding tales, they help to ease this potentially endless narrative to its rest. And I would further suggest that it is important that these are the stories of two of those ladies who sought to overturn the dominant culture in which they, as narrative-women, are embedded, for it is yet another concession to the literary, social, and political norms embodied in Harun al-Rashid.

The way in which the actual story of each of the five major tales is handled in the closing frame is significant. The three dervishes' narratives receive barely passing notice. No steps are taken to counteract their action; no attempt is made to right any of the physical wrongs committed in their course. The response to the two ladies' tales, however, is quite different. Not only is the ifrit necessary literally to undo the damage cited by the two women, but the narrative takes great pains to track this reversal in some detail. The story of the ifrit is repeated by the ifrit herself before she returns the dogs to their former human state, in much the same way that she reminds the caliph of his son's action before al-Amin can confirm it himself. Fortunately, the repeated narratives are relatively brief. The ifrit waxes fairly eloquent about her own personal history but repeats only in shortened form the story of the second lady and her jealous husband. The same narrative attitude is maintained with al-Amin: "Then the caliph, O King, summoned his son al-Amin and questioned him to confirm the truth of the story" (150).[13] The closing frame of the cycle employs in relatively concentrated fashion many of the repetitive patterns discussed in relation to the three dervishes' tales; but what the ifrit's retelling of the ladies' stories suggests is that since the structural underpinnings of the stories are themselves of little use in returning the ladies to an earlier state, since the ladies have apparently lost their metaphoric power, the story and discourse of the closing frame must compensate.

Regardless of the means, we finally arrive at the cycle's

end, which predates, in a sense, its beginning, at the point at which all of the characters (with the exception of the luckless porter, who has long disappeared from narrative sight) are restored to their former condition and forever removed from further narrative influence. I have suggested throughout this discussion that the kind of narrative movement that instigates such an ending is intimately linked to an effort to contradict and counteract the forward-moving march of time, which necessitates the kind of change and potential for revolution that the *1001 Nights* is apparently arguing against.

But this forward temporal movement also brings us all, characters and readers alike, to our natural end. One might argue that the drive of such a repetitively structured narrative is to achieve the status of the timeless, the eternal, the ultimate conservative state, and to move beyond the boundaries of beginning and end. It is a status achieved on a minimal level by every narrative in its capacity to be reread, reexperienced, repeated, at any time and place. It is, nonetheless, particularly significant in a narrative created according to the structures and restrictions of a repetitive mode. Shahrazad's own narrative is intensely aware of such time-breaking narrative potential. Not only is it structured according to the fundamental repetitive act of narration, which provides the foundation upon which the *1001 Nights* is built; but its very title accentuates the narrative drive that actualizes such potential. As Ferial Ghazoul notes, in Arabic the number one thousand (1000) connotes a number beyond count; one thousand and one (1001) suggests that final move into eternity, into the realm where the mere passing of days and nights has no significance.[14] Shahrazad tells stories for one thousand and one nights in order to move beyond time, to reassert certain deeply embedded cultural norms and patterns of literary and social behavior that are being subject against their will to alteration and reconsideration. The three ladies and their companions in Baghdad do the same.

Chapter Six

Arabesque
The Aesthetics of Narrative Repetition

Qu'est-ce qu'un thyrse? Selon le sens moral et poétique, c'est un emblème sacerdotal dans la main des prêtres et des prêtresses célébrant la divinité dont ils sont les interprètes et les serviteurs. Mais physiquement ce n'est qu'un bâton, un pur bâton, perche à houblon, tuteur de vigne, sec, dur et droit. Autour de ce bâton, dans des méandres capricieux, se jouent et folâtrent des tiges et des fleurs, celles-ci sinueuses et fuyardes, celles-là penchées comme des cloches ou des coupes renversées. Et une gloire étonnante jaillit de cette complexité de lignes et de couleurs, tendres ou éclatantes. Ne dirait-on pas que la ligne courbe et la spirale font leur cour à la ligne droite et dansent autour dans une muette adoration? Ne dirait-on pas que toutes ces corolles délicates, tous ces calices, explosions de senteurs et de couleurs, éxécutent un mystique fandango autour du bâton hiératique? . . . Ligne droite et ligne arabesque, intention et expression, roideur de la volonté, sinuosité du verbe, unité du but, variété des moyens, amalgame tout-puissant et indivisible du génie, quel analyste aura le détestable courage de vous diviser et de vous séparer?

—Baudelaire, "Le thyrse"

[L'arabesque] s'offre à ses yeux comme un labyrinthe, un dédale. Elle se complique ou se simplifie au point de défier l'écrit vulgaire. Elle dérègle, ou même inverse, du langage et de l'écrit, la fonction ordinaire, qui est la communication. . . . Elle cache sa signification profonde. Elle se propose comme une énigme.

—Jacques Berque, *A propos de l'art musulman*

I

FINALLY, it remains to locate the repetitive mode of narrative discourse within both the narrative tradition suggested by the *1001 Nights* at large and the cultural tradition in which it arises. For even if the larger structure of the *1001 Nights* works to support the oppositional temporal movement so skillfully manipulated in the cycle of "The Porter and the Three Ladies," not every cycle within the initial and final frames works specifically to the same end. In this light, it is perhaps not insignificant that the three ladies cycle unfolds in the decidedly Islamic milieu of Harun al-Rashid's Baghdad.[1]

In his article on the status of repetition in narrative, Peter Brooks describes the nature of the plot line in fiction: "Plot is a kind of arabesque or squiggle toward the end. It is like Corporal Trim's arabesque with his stick, in *Tristram Shandy*, retraced by Balzac at the start of *La Peau de chagrin* to indicate the arbitrary, transgressive, gratuitous line of narrative, its deviance from the straight line."[2] The arabesque or squiggle to which Brooks is here referring is, of course, the flourish that Corporal Trim makes when he brandishes his stick, and that Tristram reproduces pictorially in an effort to indicate the inadequacy of his verbal resources. What Brooks is suggesting in his use of this visual correspondent of the nature of plot in narrative is the unnecessary deviance from the straight line in the movement of any but the simplest narrative. But he does not consider the radical difference between the figure an arabesque makes and that made by the rather careless scrawl recorded in Sterne's novel. When Corporal Trim flourishes his stick, he invisibly traces the deviant line of the squiggle, the somewhat haphazard movement of a free-falling, free-forming line in space. The carefully patterned, entirely predictable movement of the arabesque is something quite different, however, and in its origins suggests much about the significance, intention, and effect of repetition as a narrative mode.

II

The term *arabesque* is in its essence an orientalist expression created to signify a kind of artistic motif that the West saw as indigenous to the Arab East. Derived from the Italian word *rabesco,* which was first used during the Italian Renaissance (1555) to refer to the style of a certain ornamental pattern particular to Islamic design, the word was borrowed by the English in 1611 to designate, according to Randle Cotgrave's *Dictionarie of the French and English Tongues,* "Rebeske work; a small and curious flourishing." Not coincidentally, perhaps, the term came more than two centuries later to signify both the condition of being Arabian or Arabic and, additionally, the condition of being strangely mixed or fantastic.[3] The earliest definition is the one that has taken hold and that is most pertinent here.

The rebeske work to which Cotgrave referred in the seventeenth century is the abstract linear design, fundamentally ornamental in intent, which is found covering the empty spaces of even early Islamic artifacts. Books, pottery, buildings, paintings—all in some way pay tribute to that form in which the Islamic world is said to have found its most expressive artistic manifestation.[4] The principles that underlie this visually complex form, that regulate the apparent arbitrariness of its design, are relatively simple yet restrictive. Derived from a denaturalized leaf or tendril pattern, the overall structure and movement of the arabesque are based on the fundamental premise of repetition, indeed redundancy, and correspondingly symmetry. As the foremost critic of arabesque remarks in his description of the decoration of the ninth-century mosque of Ibn Ṭūlūn: "From the freely flowing scroll, stemmed leaves with an unnatural outline emanate in both directions, then split again, and the whole regenerates itself imperceptively in a symmetrical rhythm— unequivocally arabesque."[5] The initially free-falling lines of an abstract leaf pattern diverge at a certain moment and rhythmically and reciprocally repeat each other in order to form the central palmette of the arabesque. This digressive but patterned movement is repeated and elaborated until a seemingly arbitrary point. The entire pattern is then reproduced in order to generate a kind of visual harmony and rhythm.

The foundation of the arabesque, then, is the repeat unit, the horizontal and vertical mirroring of the design which ensures its spatial perpetuation. This repetition of design necessarily occurs in a spatially restricted region, which concretely influences its outer limits; but the very rhythm that derives from this spatially determined repeated movement, the visual rhythm that characterizes the arabesque, curiously counters its spatial movement. In much the same way that narrative repetition impedes the temporally determined progress of a tale from beginning to end, the repetition of pattern in arabesque stalls, for all intents and purposes, the spatial movement of its design by turning it back on itself, by making it repeat its earlier self. What seems to be the progress of a design in space is, in fact, only the repetition, the replaying of an initially determined pattern. What seems to be the end of a design is, in fact, only another manifestation of its beginning, of a point that, given the movement of repetition, could potentially antecede its beginning.

The suggestion of such inversion, of the potentially endless repetition of design, creates a kind of spatial infinity that, as a result of its obvious affiliation with the repetitive mode, encompasses the temporal realm as well. Indeed, perhaps the most common interpretation of the arabesque reads it as reflecting a concern for the infinite and eternal over and above the transience of earthly existence, as drawing the eye of the viewer away from the things of this world toward the perception of a design that potentially repeats itself into the realm of the divine. Such an interpretation results from the fundamental presence of repetition, of, specifically, the repetition of a denaturalized, nonrepresentational vegetal pattern that itself speaks of the insignificance of the material realm. The question remains, however, as to what prompted the development of such a design, why the arabesque came to be the symbol for a particular Islamic aesthetic, and what this suggests about its narrative equivalent.

III

The issue to which one inevitably turns at this point involves the status of figuration in Islam. It is an issue which has given rise to lengthy discussion and debate in recent times and to which there is no single or final solution.[6] The extent to which figural art is present in Islam seems to vary according to historical period and artistic intent. One finds, for instance, fine examples of representational art in early private monuments or under the Shiite rule of the Fatimids. But the general scholarly consensus at this point is that although such examples can be found, although no strict and overriding injunction barring figural art in Islam can be isolated, the dominant tendency seems to be an avoidance of representation, particularly of living things, in most official or formal art, especially during the early Islamic period. The corollary to such a stricture is the development of nonrepresentational, abstract design.

The justification for such an attitude can be located in

the *Ḥadīth* "Traditions," on which Islamic practice is in part based.[7] Although the *Ḥadīth* offer no direct statement forbidding representation, no clear injunction against figural artistic activity, many do suggest the severe consequences that attend anyone who engages in the practice of making such images or who associates him- or herself with the product of such activity. One reads, for example, in one of the great collections of *Ḥadīth* that "those who will be most severely punished on the Day of Judgement are the murderer of the prophet, one who leads men astray without knowledge, and a maker of images or pictures."[8] Or, similarly: "The artists, the makers of images, will be punished at the last judgement by the decree of Allah who will inflict upon them the impossible task of breathing life into their works."[9] The attitude implicit in and consequent upon such statements is necessarily iconoclastic.

Such judgments are based upon the notion of Allah himself as supreme *muṣawwir,* "image-maker," an epithet that indicates the creative, shaping function of the divine being. However, the term is also used to designate the artist or painter, that secondary, derivative maker of images who, regardless of intention, must by virtue of the nature of the artistic act challenge the divine creative activity. Within such a context, all artistic activity, all efforts to imitate—and I use the word with its mimetic aspect in mind—in whatever fashion the original creative effort impiously mirror this very effort. A thirteenth-century commentator, explicating the *Ḥadīth* that promises that an angel will not enter a house in which there is a picture, aptly explains the matter in the following way:

> The learned authorities of our school and others hold that the painting of a picture of any living thing is strictly forbidden and is one of the great sins, because it is threatened with the above grievous punishments as mentioned in the Traditions, whether it is intended for common domestic use or not. So the making of it is forbidden under every

circumstance, because it implies a likeness to the creative activity of God.[10]

Artists sought ways to respond artistically to such limitations without forgoing their creative impulse. Legend records that one artist who lamented the restrictions placed on figural representation was told by the caliph Omar to continue to paint portraits but to make them resemble flowers; and art history records numerous examples of paintings that feature a line drawn across the necks of the individuals portrayed—clearly an effort to indicate the inanimate and therefore nonreal status of the figures. The immediate concern would seem to be an avoidance of the portrayal of animate forms, but such a concern could and would be quickly generalized into a reluctance to engage in any kind of figural representation. One obvious consequence of such artistic evasion is the development of nonfigural, nonrepresentational abstract design.

Within this climate, the arabesque develops as that form which embodies what one might claim as a fundamental principle of an Islamic aesthetic. Nonfigural and thus necessarily antimimetic, the arabesque takes as its point of departure the denatured, indeed unnatural, threads of a leaf pattern and spins a self-perpetuating, potentially infinite design. Unable to point to any external phenomenon as its representational source, the arabesque, with its ever-repeating extension of an initial pattern, can ultimately establish only itself as the element it signifies. It alone engenders itself, instigates its own unfolding, and thereby supplies the information by which the figure it makes achieves meaning. It is at once the means of signification and the thing signified.

In this lies the enigma of the arabesque. The deep signification that such a figure hides lies, as Jacques Berque notes in the passage cited as the epigraph to this chapter, in its counter to the ordinary communicative function of any system of signs. As in figurative, specifically metaphoric, language, which the arabesque in its nonfigural thrust resembles, the burden of meaning is placed not on an external point of reference but rather on the relation of one element or term to an antecedent one within the same limited system. Just as metaphor finally means through a relation of resemblance or substitution, a relation based on an essential repetition of one term by another, so does arabesque signify by virtue of its repeating pattern. There is, of course, a difference of degree. The second term of the metaphor can only incompletely repeat its first term in order to achieve meaning, while the parallel relation in the figure of arabesque comes much closer to a perfect repetition of one signifying element by another. Both systems of meaning, however, remain fundamentally self-referential, finally returning to themselves in order to attain significance. In this the enigma of arabesque and the enigma of metaphor are conjoined.

IV

At this point we are not far from the narrative mode that, as earlier discussion has indicated, grows out of a discourse that foregrounds metaphor. The metaphorically engendered repetitive mode of narrative discourse that is so clearly exemplified in the cycle of "The Porter and the Three Ladies" bears a close structural affinity to the figure of arabesque and, not surprisingly, shares in its form. The one stands in metaphoric relationship to the other. The most significant comparative component undoubtedly lies in the obvious but essential movement instigated by repetition in both forms. The repeat unit that dominates the visual design of the arabesque clearly plays a no less significant role in the overall narrative design of a work such as the three ladies cycle. The repetition that occurs on various levels of the text, the insistent return in the text to an earlier narrative or textual moment, bears a strong family resemblance to the movement of arabesque, which persists in its backward-turning, repetitive course. In both cases, the movement asserts its affiliation with the repetitive mode by countering a linear temporal progression and thereby suggesting a correspondence with an atemporal, infinite, and eternal realm.

Such more or less obvious points of contact need little elaboration. What is perhaps not as clear is the applicability of the issue of figuration vis-à-vis the repetitive narrative mode. If the implicit warning against representation strongly contributed to the development of a figure like the arabesque, perhaps it plays an equally significant role in the form that offers its narrative equivalent. I am not suggesting here that the avoidance of representation in Islamic art instigated in a direct fashion the growth of a narrative structure based on repetition. I am suggesting rather that the issue of figuration, the question of the status of representation within such a mode, provides a valuable lens for viewing the larger kind of narrative that this mode produces.

I would suggest that the narrative correspondent to the rejection of artistic figuration is the development of a fundamentally antimimetic impulse, an impulse that a cycle such as that of the three ladies manifests most strongly. One need only remember the presence of magic and fantastic spaces and swords, the plethora of jinn and metamorphosed agents, indeed the general presence of women and men and environments that seemingly exceed all ordinary human norms and limits, to ascertain the decidedly nonrealist tendency of the cycle. One is here unquestionably within the realm of the marvelous, that sphere within which events contrary to or simply different from the laws and limits of the universe as we know it can and do occur. Much as the arabesque manifests its first avoidance of representation in the implicit movement away from the imitation of a leaf pattern toward the development of its denaturalized, unreal form, so does a similarly oriented narrative present a universe that bears only a faint resemblance to that within which the reader moves. We take it for granted, simply put, that the world of the three ladies and their companions, albeit in Baghdad, has no real connection with our own.

There is, upon reading the text, the dominant impression that its intention is not the more or less faithful imitation of a commonly defined reality but rather the creation of a universe that can only take root elsewhere. Such an intention is not evidenced solely in the lack of correspondence between the reader's world and that of the three ladies, in the purely imaginary, rather magical elements and characters that combine to create this narrative—though these are undeniably the most obvious manifestations of what seems to be an essentially nonrepresentational narrative. As with the arabesque, this antimimetic aspect is importantly supplemented by and grounded in the structure of its narrative, the very patterns of repetition that define the movement of the work; and just as the repeat unit of the arabesque ultimately points to the self-referential nature of the figure's movement and meaning, so do the persistent repetitions on the level of story and discourse turn the narrative back on itself, point to its fundamentally narrative source.

Indeed, the very movement of a repetitively structured narrative such as the three ladies cycle indicates its essentially antimimetic thrust, its refusal to acknowledge anything outside itself as its generating source. Ibn Sīnā (Avicenna), the great medieval Arab philosopher, pertinently remarks in his work on rhetoric that "the imaginative representation is an acceptance of the astonishment and delight in the discourse itself, while the objective presentation is an acceptance of the object just as it is said to be. Thus the imaginative representation is created by the locution itself."[11] The insistent textual returns and repetitions, the constant reminders within the narrative of an earlier textual existence, speak of nothing so much as the primacy of the narrative's discourse and the textual basis of the narrative as its point of reference. The writing of the text, its discourse, creates the realm within which the textual reality subsists. The narrative's meaning lies finally in what it points to. It inheres in the narrative and verbal fabric of the text.

V

We return for the last time to the frame story and the lesson it teaches. We learned there that within this narrative universe, metaphor delivers language from its referential function and refashions the reality this language signifies. A metaphorically generated narrative extends the structure and intent of metaphor in order to create its own narrative foundation, which repeats the same lesson. What the arabesquelike design of the cycle of "The Porter and the Three Ladies" tells of is the power of repetition in narrative to induce a self-generated, textually grounded work that has little referential value outside itself. The result is not unlike those figural depictions found in Islamic art which are nothing more than the calligraphic manipulation of letters and words. The meaning of the sign lies not in the object to which it refers but in the words that give it body.

The three ladies cycle provides one of the finest examples of this kind of narrative. Fundamentally repetitive in structure and metaphoric in orientation, the cycle nonetheless plays with the repetitive mode to varying degrees and in so doing underscores the potential of its effect. There is, in fact, a kind of buildup in the development of such a mode. The frame story, as always, stands apart, for in both its opening and closing aspects, it provides in miniature the perfect example of the kind of narrative toward which the embedded stories of the cycle move. The three dervishes' stories progress incrementally in respect to the degree to which repetitive structures are manipulated, the third dervish's tale maximalizing the possibilities of such structures. The two ladies then take over and provide a gradual attenuation of the techniques of repetition and, as discussed above, bring the cycle to its close.

What is worth noting in this progression is the extent to which the varying presence of repetition influences the kind of story told. A tale such as that of the first dervish, or even more noticeably, the second lady, tales that exercise the potential of repetition very little if at all, are decidedly less marvelous or fantastic in impulse than the others. The political disturbance that befalls the first dervish, the loss of his eye and his exile from his homeland, the accident that besets his cousin, however bizarre, are only slightly more strange than the events in the second lady's tale, which unremarkably tells a story of domestic unhappiness. The other tales, by contrast, all of which manipulate structures of repetition to a greater degree, are far more challenging to the reader's credibility in their depiction of a world that pays little attention to the laws of our own. Radical metamorphoses, the animation of the inanimate, the endless and exact multiplication of a seemingly single character, the discovery of a petrified city—all and more attest to the atmosphere of a waking dream, to the strongly nonmimetic, antirealist aspect of the various tales. Those tales that most strongly manifest a nonrepresentational bias, the tales of the second and especially the third dervish, are the ones in which the patterns of repetition are most pervasive and complex. If, in the end, the cycle is returned to the real world of Harun al-Rashid and all that this implies, it is not for want of trying to do otherwise.

The *1001 Nights* is commonly remembered as that collection of tales which specializes in this nonrepresentational bias. Popular memory records the fabulous treasures and beautiful women, the magical palaces and bottled jinn, which have typically come to represent the world that belongs to the *Nights;* but to associate only this with such an extensive narrative universe is to underestimate its breadth and diversity. Tales of "The Porter and the Three Ladies" variety are indeed prominent in this collection and are particularly noticeable in those cycles that are propelled by storytelling activity. One must not ignore, however, those cycles that have little access to this realm, sequences such as that of Nur al-Din Ali or Ali al-Zi'baq, which are prototypically realist in the way the nineteenth-century novelistic tradition has allowed us to define the term. Such stories depict in a remarkably objective fashion attitudes, customs, practices of a specific, historically limited segment of society. The narrative intention would seem to be, in the words of Ibn Sīnā, the objective presentation of the object just as it is said to be, rather than the imaginative representation of the locution itself. Such cycles unfold in a decidedly straightforward, linear fashion, using only such minimal structures of repetition as are necessary to the development of any narrative. In another world and time, it would be useful for an understanding of the way the larger narrative universe of the *1001 Nights* as a whole is constructed to juxtapose these seemingly oppositional narrative worlds and the materials needed to build them. For this time, however, we must leave these straight lines and arabesques to define in their ever-shifting fashion the textual realm of the *1001 Nights*.

Notes

Chapter One

1. Quoted by Littmann in his article "Alf Layla wa-Layla," in *Encyclopedia of Islam.*

2. *The Arabian Nights Entertainment,* ed. ul Yumunee (Calcutta, 1814, 1818); *Tausend und eine Nacht,* ed. Habicht; *Kitāb Alf Laylah wa-Laylah,* ed. al-Sharqāwī (the so-called Bulaq ed.); *The Alif Laila or the Book of the Thousand Nights and One Night,* ed. Macnaghten (Calcutta, 1839–42).

3. *The 1001 Nights (Alf Layla wa-Layla) from the Earliest Known Sources,* ed. Mahdi.

4. For a thorough discussion of this topic, see the articles by MacDonald and Mahdi cited in the Bibliography, particularly Mahdi's introduction to his edition of *Alf Layla wa-Layla.* For a general view of the various manuscripts and printed editions, the above-cited article in the *Encyclopedia of Islam* is quite useful, as is the introduction by Haddawy to his recent translation of the Mahdi edition.

5. Borges, "The Thousand and One Nights." The most recent translation of *The Arabian Nights* by Haddawy provides the exception to this rule. It is telling that this is the first time that the text has been translated into a Western language by an Arab.

6. Ghazoul, *The Arabian Nights;* Gerhardt, *The Art of Story-Telling.*

7. Hamori, *On the Art of Medieval Arabic Literature;* Miquel, *Ajib et Gharib;* Miquel, *Sept contes des "Milles et une nuits."*

8. See, e.g., in Ghazoul: "The metaphoric nature of the matrix corresponds to the intensive use of metaphors in the entire discourse of Shahrazad, where the story seems something of a poetic narrative" (p. 52) (though, interestingly, Ghazoul associates the metonym with the cycle of "The Porter and the Three Ladies"). And, "While in folklore, reworking of motifs is common, *The Arabian Nights* is distinctive for its repetition more than reworking, with the result that the corpus produces the effect of a merry-go-round where every once in a while one rider comes to the front and then soon disappears to be replaced by another" (p. 131). I have found Ghazoul's work particularly illuminating for the way it confirms some of my own findings and points the way for further development.

9. Todorov, "Les hommes-récits."

10. See esp. Jakobson, *Language in Literature;* Todorov, *Poétique de la prose;* Genette, *Figures III;* Brooks, "Freud's Masterplot"; Miller, *Fiction and Repetition;* and Deleuze, *Différence et répétition.*

Chapter Two

1. *The Book of the Thousand Nights and a Night,* trans. Burton. The Kufic script reads *Kitāb Alf Laylah,* "The Book of a Thousand Nights."

2. See, most notably, Todorov, "Les hommes-récits."

3. Unless otherwise indicated, all translations from "The Story of the Porter and the Three Ladies" are from Haddawy's recent translation, *The Arabian Nights,* and all references to the Arabic text of this cycle are drawn from Mahdi's edition, *Kitāb Alf Laylah wa-Laylah.* The original Arabic is given in the notes.

4.

صرفاً كان سناها ضوّ مقباسى	١ ناولتها شبه خذّيها معتقةً
فكيف تهدى خدود الناس للناسى	٢ فقبلتها وقالت وهى ضاحكةً
دمى وصابفها بالكاس انفاسى	٣ قلت اشربى فهى من دمى وحمرتها
فاسقنيها عل العينين والراسى (١٢٢)	قالت فان كنت من اجلى بكيت دماً

5.

وما زالوا كدالك حتى سكروا ولعبت الخمره فى عقولهم. فلما ان تحكم الشراب قامت البوابه الى البحره وتجردت من تيابها وبقيت عريانه زلط وارخت شعرها عليها سترها وقالت شكّ نزلت الى البحره فنطست وتغسلت ولعبت وبطبطت واخدت من الماء فى فمها وبخت عليهم تم غسلت تحت نهودها

124

وغسلت ما بين فخديها وداخل صرتها وطلعت بسرعه من البحره وقعدت في حجر الحمال
وقالت له سيعي، حبيبي، ايش هو هده - وحطت يدها على حرها - فقالت للحمال ايش هو هده. قال
رحمك. قالت واه واه، ما تستحي، ونزلت في رقبته. فقال فرجك. والاخرى صرخت ونطلته وقالت وه
قبيح. قال كسكي، والاخرى لكمته في صدره اقلبته وقالت يوه استحي. قال زنبورك. فضربته العريانه
وقالت لا. قال هنكي، دندولكي، ودنيكتكي. قالت لا لا. فبقى كلما يقول شى تلكمه واحده من البنات
وتقول ما اسمه هده. فصارت دى تلكمه ودى تضربه ودى تنطله. قال يا اخي ما اسمه. قالت اسمه حبق
الجسور. فقال الحمال حبق الجسور، وما كان هده من الاول، اه اه. تم دار الكاس بينهم ساعه وقامت
الحوشكاشه تجردت من جميع اثوابها كما فعلت اختها البوابه وقالت شك، غطست فى البحره وربطبطت
وغسلت تحت بطنها وحوالى نهودها وغسلت ما بين افخادها وطلعت بسرعه ووقعت فى حجر الحمال
وقالت سويد قلبي، ايش هو دا. قال فرجك. وهى نخلته [نخله] طنت لها القاعه وقالت يوه ما تستحي.
قال رحمك. فضربته اختها وقالت افوه قبيح. قال زنبورك. فلكمته اختها وقالت وه وه، ما فيك حيا.
فبقت دى تلكمه ودى تلطمه ودى تضربه ودى تنخله وهو يقول رحمك، كسك، دندولك، ودندلك لا
لا. قال حبق الجسور، والتلاته ضحكوا حتى انقلبوا، ونزلوا التلاته فى رقبته جمله واحده وقالوا لا، ما
هو / اسمه. قال يا اخي فايش اسمه. قالت ما تقول السمسم المقشور. قال الحمد لله على السلامه،
السمسم المقشور. تم لبست الجاريه قماشها وجلسوا يتنادموا والحمال يتاره من رقبته واكتافه. فدار
الكاس بينهم ساعه. وقامت الكبيره مليحتهم تجردت من قماشها، فسك الحمال رقبته بيده ومرجها وقال
فى سبيل الله رقبتى واكتافي. تم تعرت الصبيه والقت نفسها فى البحره ثم غطست. فنظر الحمال الى
الصبيه عريانه كانها فلقه قمر، بوجه كانه البدر ادا ابدر والصبح ادا اسفر، ونظرها والى قدها ونهدها والى
تلك الارداف الثقال الذى تترجرج وهى عريانه كما خلقها ربها، فقال اه اه، وانشد يخاطبها شعر (٢٠):

١ ان قست قدك بالغصن الرطيب فقد   حملت قلبى اوزاراً وريهتانا

٢ فالغصن احسن ما تلقاه متزرأً   وانت احسن ما نلقاك عريانا

فلما سمعت الصبيه شعره طلعت بسرعه وقعدت فى حجر الحمال وارمت الى حرها وقالت يا عوينتى، يا
كبيدتى، ايش اسم هده. قال حبق الجسور. قالت وه. قال السمسم المقشور. قالت افه. قال رحمك.
قالت يوه، ما تستحي، ونزلت فى رقبته. فقال فرجك. وما اطيل على الملك، الا ان الحمال بقى يقول لها اسمه كدى
وهى تقول لا لا لا لا. بعد ما اكل سك وقرص وعض حتى ورمت رقبته وانخنق وكرب قال يا اخي فايش
اسمه. قالت ما تقول خان ابو مسرور. قال الحمال هاها، خان ابو مسرور. فقامت لبست اثوابها وعادوا
الى ما كانوا عليه ودار الكاس بينهم ساعه. (٥_١٢٢)

6. *Thousand Nights and a Night*, trans. Burton, 1:92.

7. Abu Deeb, *al-Jurjāni's Theory of Poetic Imagery*, p. 75.

8.

امرأة ملتفه فى ايزار موصلى مشعر بحرير بعمصه قلعيه بخف ذرخونى بشريط لاعب بسرموجه بعرق
لاعب، (٧_١٢٦) فوقعت عليه وشالت شعريتها بان من تحتها عيون سود بهدب اجفان طوال مدنبه ناعمة الاطراف
كاملة الاوصاف، كما قال فيها بعض واصفيها

9.

يا اختى ايش تستنوا، ادخلوا من الباب وحطى عن هدا المسكين. (١٢٩)

10.

فنظر الحمال من فتح لها الباب وادا بها صبية خماسية القد قاعدة النهد، دات حسن وجمال ويهاء وكمال
وقد واعتدال، بجبين كفرة الهلال وعيون تحاكى عيون المها والغزلان وحاجب كهلال شعبان وخدود
كشقايق النعمان وفم كخاتم سليمان وشفيفات حمر كالعقيان وسنينات كلولو منضد فى مرجان وعنق كانه
حشيشانكه قدمت للسلطان وصدر كانه شادروان ونهود كانهن فحلين رمان وبطن مع سره تسع نصف
اوقيه من دهن البان وهنا كراس ارنب مقطش الاردان، كما قال فيه الشاعر اللسان (٢١):

١ انظر الى شمس القصور وبدرها   والى خزاماها وبهجة زهرها

٢ لم تلق عينك ابيض فى اسود   جمع الجمال كوجهها مع شعرها

٣ محمرة الوجنات تخبر حسنها   عن اسمها اد لم تحيط بخبرها

٤ وتمايلت فضحكت من اردافها   عجباً ولكنى بكيت لخصرها   (٩ـ١٢٨)

11. In the *Rhetoric*, trans. Roberts, p. 173, Aristotle notes: "The Simile is also a metaphor; the difference is but slight."

12.

صبية بطلعة مضيه وبهجة رضيه واخلاق فيلسوفيه بخلقه قمريه وعيون بابليه وحواجب قسى محنيه وقامه الفيه ونكهه عنبريه وشفيفات سكريه وطره بهج تخجل الشمس المضيه كانها بعض الكواكب العلويه او قبة دهب مبنيه او عروسه مجليه او بلطيه فى فسقيه او ليه فى لبنيه، كما فيها الشاعر قال (٢٢):

١ كانما تبسم عن لولوء   منضد او برد او اقاح

٢ وطرة كالليل مرخية   وبهجة تخجل ضو الصباح   (١٢٩)

13. The phrase is Paul Ricoeur's. It is taken from the essay "The Metaphorical Process as Cognition," p. 151.

14. Abu Deeb, *al-Jurjānī's Theory of Poetic Imagery*, p. 77.

15. The full passage as translated by Abu Deeb reads: "By al-maʿna I mean what you understand from the immediate expression, and what you reach without a special medium. By maʿna al-maʿna I mean that you comprehend a certain meaning from the expression, and the meaning leads you to another meaning."

16. See Heinrichs, *The Hand of the North-Wind*, p. 7. Heinrichs notes that "*tamthīl* and *ḍarb mathal* are used synonymously by such a conscientious scholar as al-Jurjānī, who otherwise is very prone to making subtle distinctions."

17. Pellat, "Kināya," in *Encyclopedia of Islam*.

18. Aristotle, *Rhetoric*, trans. Roberts, p. 170. See also the *Poetics*, trans. Bywater, p. 24.

19. Brooke-Rose, *Grammar of Metaphor*, p. 24.

20.

وقام الحمال فتجرد من اترابه جميعها فتدلا شى من بين افخاده، ونط وصار فى وسط البحره ثم طلع بسرعه وتلقف فى حجر المليحه وارمى ادرعته فى حجر البوابه ورجليه وسيقانه فى حجر الحوشكاشه وقال يا ستاه ايش هده، راومى الى ايره. فتضاحكوا واعجبهم فمايله اد هو حاز الطرب منهم وطباعه قابل طباعهم. فقالت الواحده زبك. فقال ما تستحوا، قبيح. قالت اخرى ايرك. قال استحوا قبحكم الله. قالت الاخرى زبرتك. [قال لا.] قالوا نهدك. قال لا. قالوا شيك، خصوك، محشك. قال الحمال لا جلا لا. قالوا ايش اسم هده. وهو قد باس هده وخرطم هده وقرص دى وعض دى وقطم على دى واخد غرته منهم، والبنات قد انقلبوا من الضحك على فعله وقالوا له يا اخونا ما اسمه. قال الحمال ما تعرفوا اسمه، هده البغل الكسور. قالوا ايش معنى اسمه البغل الكسور. قال الدى يرعى حبق الجسور ويسف السمسم المقشور ويبرطع فى خان ابو مسرور. فضحكوا وانقلبوا من الضحك حتى غشى عليهم   (٦ـ١٢٥)

21. Cohen, "Metaphor and the Cultivation of Intimacy," p. 6.

22. Ibid., p. 7.

23. "Apparently Arab scholars, when speaking of the text, use this admirable expression: *the certain body.*" Barthes, *Le plaisir du texte,* p. 29 (English translation from *The Pleasure of the Text,* trans. Richard Miller [New York, 1975], p. 16).

24.

يا اختاه افهمى ما اوصيكى به، انا ادا طلعت الى السلطان ارسل وراكى فادا طلعتى ورايتى الملك قضا حاجته قولى لى يا اختاه ان كنتى غير نايمه فحدثينى حدوته، فها انا احدثكم فهى سبب نجاتى وخلاص هده الامه   (٧١)

25. *Thousand Nights and a Night,* trans. Burton, 9:272.

26. Wright in *Grammar of the Arabic Language,* 3:19, explains the rule of *iḍāfah* in the following way:

> The idea of one noun is very often more closely determined or defined by that of another. When this is the case, the noun so defined is shortened in its pronunciation by the omission of the tanwin, or of the terminations and . . . on account of the speaker's passing on rapidly to the determining word, which is put in the genitive. The determined noun is called by the Arab grammarians *al-muḍāfu,* the annexed; the determining noun *al-muḍāfu ilayhi,* that to which annexation is made or to which another word is annexed; and the relation subsisting between them is known as *al-iḍāfa,* the annexation. European grammarians are accustomed to say that the determined or governing word is in the *status constructus.*

27. Ricoeur, "Metaphorical Process as Cognition," p. 142.

28.

[ايتها] الست تعلمى ان سبب مجيى اننى رجل حمال حملتنى هده الحوشكاشه وجيت من بيت النباد الى دكان الجزار ومن الجزار الى البياع ومن البياع الى الفاكهانى ومن الفاكهانى الى النقل والحلوائى والعطار وجيت الى هده الدار وهده حديتى   (١٤٨)

Chapter Three

1. This point has been made by Todorov in his essay "Les hommes-récits." It is worth remarking, though, that narrative does not always attain its desired goal. The interpolated exemplary tale of "The Envier and the Envied" in another version of this cycle provides one example of a narrative that fails in its purpose; the

"reeve's tale" and the "Tale of the Jewish Doctor" in the Hunchback cycle offer two other examples of failed narrative.

2.

وقالت كلمن احكى لنا حكايه وما جرى له وما سبب مجيه عندنا خلوه يملس على راسه ويخرج يروح الى حال سبيله، ومن ابى اضربوا رقبته (١٤٧)

3. "A character is a potential story that is the story of his life. Every new character signifies a new plot. We are in the realm of narrative-men." Todorov, "Les hommes-récits," p. 37 (English translation from *The Poetics of Prose,* trans. Richard Howard [New York, 1977], p. 70).

4. "Embedding is an articulation of the most essential property of all narrative. For the embedding narrative is the *narrative of a narrative.* By telling the story of another narrative, the first narrative achieves its fundamental theme and at the same time is reflected in this image of itself." Ibid., p. 40 (p. 72).

5.

وحياتكم انى امرءٌ لبيب عاقلاً اديب، قراءت العلوم وحزت الفهوم، قريت ودريت واسندت وارويت، اظهر الجميل واكتم القبيح ولا يبدو منى الا كل مليح، وانا كما قال القايل (٢٥):

١ ما يكتم السرَّ الا كل ذى ثقة   والسر عند خيار الناس مكتومُ
٢ السرَّ عندى فى بيتٍ لهُ غلقٌ   قد ضاع مفتاحهُ والقفل مختومُ (١٢١)

6.

فقال الحمال وانتم يا اخواننا ما معكم فضيله تبدوها (١٢٧)

7.

وكان سبب دق الباب ان تلك الليله نزل فيها هرون الرشيد الخليفه وجعفر الى المدينه وكانت هده عادتهم كل قليل. فلما شقوا تلك الليله المدينه كانت جوازهم من على الباب، فسمعوا حس موصول وجنك ودق وصراخ البنات بالغنا ومنادمه وضحك. (١٢٨)

8.

يا سيدتاه نحن تجار مواصله ـ من اهل الموصل ـ ولنا فى هده المدينه عشرة ايام (١٢٩)

9.

قالوا له ما تبات عندنا الا بشرط تدخل تحت الحكم والرضى، ومهما رايت منا او فينا لا تسال عن سببه، ولا تتكلم فيما لا يعنيك تسمع ما لا يرضيك، فهده شرطنا معك، لا تكثر فضولك ادا رايت شيأ عملناه. فقال نعم نعم نعم، وانا بلا لسان ولا عين. فقالوا له قم واقرى ما على الباب والدهليز. فقام واتى الى الباب وقرا فوجد مكتوب على الباب والدهليز بما الدهب المحلول «من تكلم فيما لا يعنيه سمع ما لا يرضيه». قال الحمال اشهدكم على انى لا اتكلم فيما لا يعنينى. فاشرطوا عليه دلك. (١٢٦)

10. The poem displays the porter's poetic gifts at their lowest ebb. Not surprisingly, the women's response is laughter.

11. Brooks, "Freud's Masterplot," p. 291. Brooks notes the importance of Said's work *Beginnings* in this regard.

12. Ibid., p. 281.

13.

فتقدم الحمال وقال يا ستاه ان هاولاى الجماعه قالوا [مرادهم] ان يحبوا ان تحدثيهم بحديث هولاى الكلبتين السود وكيف انتى تعاقبيهم وتدورى تبكى عليهم، وخبر اختكى وكيف ضربها بالقارع مثل الرجال، لا غير ولا سوى، هدا مرادهم. (١٤٦)

14. "Where there is no succession, there is no narrative." Bré-mond, "La logique des possibles narratifs," p. 68 (my translation).

15. Barthes, "Introduction à l'analyse structurale des récits," p. 16.

16. Jakobson, "Two Aspects of Language," p. 255.

17. Jakobson, "Linguistics and Poetics," p. 370: "In poetry where similarity is superinduced upon contiguity, any metonymy is slightly metaphorical and any metaphor has a metonymical tint."

18. Brooks, "Freud's Masterplot," pp. 280–81.

19. Todorov, "La quête du récit."

20. Lord, *Singer of Tales*.

21. Benjamin, "The Image of Proust," in *Illuminations*, p. 204.

22. Jakobson, "Two Aspects of Language," p. 258.

23. Jakobson, "Linguistics and Poetics," p. 371.

24. Boas, *Primitive Art*, p. 39.

25. "An event is not only capable of happening; it can also happen again, or be repeated: the sun rises every day." Genette, *Figures III*, p. 145 (English translation from *Narrative Discourse: An Essay in Method*, trans. Jane E. Lewin [Ithaca, N.Y., 1980], p. 113).

Chapter Four

1. This is Edward Said's concept of repetition as filiation. See Said, in "On Repetition," in *The World, the Text, and the Critic*. In his primary discussion of the repetition compulsion in *Beyond the Pleasure Principle*, trans. Strachey, p. 31, Freud discusses this notion and remarks that "the most impressive proofs of there being an organic compulsion to repeat lie in the phenomena of heredity and the facts of embryology. We see how the germ of a living animal is obliged in the course of its development to recapitulate (even if

only in a transient and abbreviated fashion) the structures of all the forms from which it is sprung."

2. "The 'repetition' is in fact a mental construction, which eliminates from each occurrence everything belonging to it that is peculiar to itself, in order to preserve only what it shares with all the others of the same class, which is an abstraction: . . . This is well known, and I recall it only to specify once and for all that what we will name here 'identical events' or 'recurrence of the same event' is a series of several similar events *considered only in terms of their resemblance.*" Genette, *Figures III,* p. 145 (trans. Lewin, p. 113).

3. Suleiman, *Authoritarian Fictions,* pp. 149–97.

4. Rimmon-Kenan, "Paradoxical Status of Repetition," p. 152.

5. Miller, *Fiction and Repetition,* p. 3.

6. Ibid., pp. 5–6.

7. "Whether competition or translation, realist simulation is still, or already, a variation on this same imposed, that is to say agreed upon, theme that one calls History, society, truth, Happiness, lost Time, who knows what all, and that the most 'faithful' representation calls us, now without digression, to *ricercare.*" Genette, "L'autre du même," p. 13 (my translation).

8. Lawlor, "Event and Repeatability," p. 329. Lawlor is here referring to Derrida's argument regarding the repeatability of the spoken element.

9. ". . . that almost institutional practice of classical Arab-Islamic culture: the evening conversation. . . . The *samar* is usually what brings the working day to a close before a night's sleep; and there is every reason to think that the storyteller's *samar* relates to that form, which we imagine him practicing among a small group or in the public square." Miquel, *Ajib et Gharib,* pp. 225–26 (my translation).

10.

يا ابن اخى اخبرك ان هذا ولدى من صغره قد تولع بحب اخته، وكنت انهاه عن ذلك واقول فى نفسى "هؤلاى صغار". (١٥٢)

11.

تم احكيت لها ما جرى على فالها ذلك وقالت وانا الاخرى اعلمك بقصتى (١٠٨

12.

يا سيدتاه، فلما سالت الصبى عن قصته وتحقق انى من جنسه فرح ورد لونه وقربنى اليه وقال يا اخى
قصتى عجيبه وحكايتى غريبه   (٤_١٨٢)

13.

على الباب الساعه ثلاث رجال قرندليه عوران كل واحد منهم محلوق الراس والدقن والحواجب مقلوع
العين اليمين، وهذه من اعجب الاتفاقات،   (١٢٧)

14.

والدى كان ملك وله اخ والاخ ملك   (١٤٨)

15.

وانما اعلمك انتى كنت ابن ملك. وعلمنى والدى الخط والقران   (١٥٥)

16.

ما قصتى كقصتهم وان حديثى اغرب واعجب وهو سبب قلع عينى وحلق دقنى. وذلك ان هؤلاءِ رفقاتيي
جاهم القضا والقدر بغته وانا الذى جلبت القضا بيدى وجلبت الهم لروحى.   (١٧٨)

17.

اى كان ملك عظيم الشان قوى السلطان.   (٩_١٧٨)

18

وخرجت من المدينه ولا عرفنى احداً وقصدت هذه البلاد وسلكت هذه الطريق على انى اقصد مدينه بغداد
لعل يسعدنى دهرى واجد من يوصلنى الى امير المومنين وخليفة رب العالمين، حتى ابت له قصتى وما
جرى على ناصيتى. فوصلت الى باب المدينه فى هذه الليله ووقفت حايراً لا ادرى الى اين امضى وادا هذا
القرندلى الذى الى جائى قد اقبل وعليه اثر السفر، فسلم فقلت له اغريب انت. قال نعم. [فقلت] وانا
كذلك. فنحن فى الحديث وهذا الذى بجانبنا وهو القرندلى الاخر قد ادركنا فى الباب فسلم علينا وقال
غريب. قلنا له ونحن كذالك. فتمشينا وقد هجم علينا [الليل] ونحن غربا ما نحن نعرف اين نسلك،
(١٥٢_٤)

19.

ثم انى سافرت الاقطار ودرت الامصار وقصدت بغداد لعى اتوصل بمن يوقفنى بين يدى امير المومنين
فاعلمه بقصتى وما جرى على ناصيتى، وجيت فى هذه الليله فوجدت اخى هذا واقف فسلت عليه وقلت
غريب. فقال غريب. فما لبثنا غير مساعه حتى اتانا هذه الاخر فسلم علينا وقال غريب. فقلنا ونحن
غربا مثلك. فمشينا وقد هجم الليل علينا فساقتنا القدره اليكم والقدوم عليكم.   (١٧٨)

20.

وكتب الله على بالسلامه فوصلت الى بغداد فى اول هذه الليله فاجد هاولاى الاثنين واقفين حايرين
فسلمت عليهم وقلت غريب. قالوا غريب، ونحن غربا. واتفق لنا ان نحن الثلاثه قرندليه عوران كل من
اليمين فصرنا اعجوبه.   (١٩١)

21.

اقبل على عشر شبان نقيين الاثواب ومعهم شيخ كبير، الا ان الشباب عوران كل شاب منهم مقلوع عينه
اليمين فعجبت لقصتهم ولاتفاقهم فى عورهم.   (١٨٩)

22.

فخرجت الى المقابر والجبانه وفتشت على التربه فلم اعرفها ولم اعرف خبرها. فما زلت ادور تربه تربه
وقبر قبر الى ان اقبل الليل . . . فجيت الدار اكلت شى ونمت منقلباً الى الصباح، فرحت الى الجبانه
وقد افتكرت جميع ما فعلته وفعله هو، وفتشت ودورت حتى دخل الليل فلم اجد التربه ولا عرفت لها

طريق . فعاودت يوماً تالتاً ويوماً رابعاً وانا افتش من بكرة النهار الى الليل فلم اعرف للتربه طريق ،
فزاد بى الوسواس والغبون حتى كدت ان اخرج مجنون   (٥-١٤٩)

23.

ثم انه اشترى لى فاساً وحبلاً وسلمنى لبعض الدين يحتطبون الحطب فخرجت معهم واحتطبت نهارى كله
واتيت بحمله على راسى فبعتها بنصف دينار فاتيت به الى الخياط. واقمت على هده مدة سنة كامله.
(١٥٧)

24.

وبعد السنه انا يوم من الايام ودخلت البريه واستغرقت فيها فوجدت غوطة اشجار وروضة انهار وما
جارى، فدخلتها فوجدت اصل شجره فبحت بالفاس حولها وازلت التراب فوجدت حلقه وادا هى فى طابق
خشب (١٥٧)

25. For the sake of clarity, I am relying throughout this section, except where indicated, on literal translations of the Arabic. Haddawy's translation understandably avoids such heavy-handed repetition.   فبكيت بكاء شديداً (١٥١)

26.

وبكا بكا شديد   (١٥١)

27.

ففرح فرحاً شديداً   (١٥١)

28.

ففرحت انا الاخر فرحاً شديد   (١٥١)

29.

وضرب بها وجه ولده ضرباً وجيعاً   (١٥٢)

30.

فبكيت بكاء شديداً على ما جرى على حتى على ابكيته   (١٥٠)

31.

يا تجار هده القرد قد استجار بى وقد اجرته   (١٦٦)

32.

تم قدمت له شياً من الاكل فاكلنا ، تم قمت   (١٨٥)

33.

فقلعتني اتوابى وقلعت هى اتوابها   (١٥٩)

34.

ونام ... ونمت   (١٨٥)

35.

فخرجت الى المقابر والجبانه وفتشت على التربه . . . فما زلت ادور تربه تربه وقبر قبر الى ان اقبل
الليل . . . فرحت الى الجبانه . . . ودورت حتى دخل الليل . . . فعاودت يوماً تالتاً ويوماً رابعاً
وانا افتش من بكرة النهار الى اليل فلم اعرف للتربه طريق ،   (٥-١٤٩)

36. Occasionally, the repetition is only implied. The narrator establishes the basic movement of an action that is to be repeated over a period of time and then indicates its repetition through the use of a resumptive phrase. For example, the third dervish describes the life he leads with the beautiful youth for a period of forty days in the following manner:

> Then I offered him something to eat, and after the two of us ate I rose and cut pieces of wood for checkers and set the pieces on the checkerboard. We diverted and amused ourselves, playing and eating and drinking till nightfall. Then I rose, lit the lamps, and offered him some sweets, and after we ate and savored some, we sat and chatted, then went to sleep.
>
> My lady, in this way we passed many days and nights. . . . (120)

37.

فقمت وفتحت الخزانة الاولى ودخلتها فوجدت فيها بستان كانه الجنه وفيه من جميع الفواكه والاثمار، اشجار باسقه واثمار يانعه ... ثم خرجت من البستان وغلقت بابه. فلما كان من الغد فتحت باباً اخر ودخلت فوجدته ميداناً كبيراً وفيه نخلاً كثيراً وبدايره نهراً جارياً ... ثم خرجت منه وغلقت بابه. وفتحت باباً ثالثاً فوجدت فيها قاعه كبيره مجزعه بانواع الرخام الملون والمعادن الثمينه والفصوص الفاخره ... ونت واصبحت وفتحت باباً رابعاً فوجدته بيتاً كبيراً وفي البيت اربعين خزانه بداير البيت مفتوحه الابواب فدخلت جميع الخزاين ووجدت فيهم من اللولو والزمرد والجوهر والياقوت والمرجان والبهرمان والمعادن والفضه والدهب ... ولم ازل يا سيدتي على مثل ذلك ايام وليالي وانا اتفرج الى ان مضت تسعه وتلاثون يوماً وبقى يوم وليله وقد فتحت الابواب والخزاين تسعه وتسعون خزانه وبقيت تمام الماىه التى اوصوني ان لا افتحها ... وغلب على الشيطان وفتحت الباب المصفح بالدهب فدخلت فاجد فيه راىحةً (١٩٦–١٩٨)

38. This condition is verbally placed upon the porter, who in turn repeats it after reading it and then places it upon the dervishes. The women in turn place it upon the caliph, who is reminded of the oath by Ja'far. And finally, the women restate the condition to all their guests one last time just before requesting their stories.

«لا يتكلموا فيما لا يعنيكم يسمعوا ما لا يرضيكم.» (١٢٧)

39.

لو كتب بالابر على اماق البصر كان عبرةً لمن اعتبر (١٤٧)

40. The opening of the frame story is, in fact, structured upon the verbal and performative repetition of the acts of buying, carrying, and following.

Chapter Five

1. See Kawin, *Telling It Again and Again,* p. 7.

2.

فساقتنا الى داركم المقادير، فانعمتم واتصدقتم بدخولنا اليكم وقد انسيت قلع عينى وحلق دقنى فقالت الصبيه ملس على راسك وروح. فقال والله لابرحت حتى اسمع ما جرى لغيرى ... دكروا ايها الملك السعيد ان القرندلى الاول تعجبوا الحاضرين من كلامه، وقال الخليفه لجعفر هدا اعجب ما سمعته فى عمرى. ثم تقدم القرندلى الثانى وقال (١٥٤)

3.

تم تقدم اول قرندلى وقال لاعلمك ايتها الست سبب قلع عينى وحلق دقنى. ودلك ان والدى كان ملك وله اخ والاخ ملك (١٤٨)

4.

وله غايب عنى مدة اربع ايام وقد بقى ستة ايام لقدومه الى عندى، فهل لك ان تقيم عندى خمسة ايام وتنصرف قبل مجيه بيوم. (١٥٩)

5. Brooks, "Freud's Masterplot," p. 286.

6. See Todorov's discussion of this issue in "La grammaire du récit."

7.

ازوج البنتين الدى كانوا مسحورين والصبيه الاولى اختهم ازوج التلاته للتلاته قرندليه اولاد الملوك (٢١٨)

8. Grossman, "Infidelity and Fiction," p. 114. I have found Grossman's article particularly suggestive for the terms in which she discusses the problem of women's selfhood and subjectivity in the *Nights.*

9. The two meanings of the word *corpus* again intersect. Richard Burton most demonstrably suggests this etymological conjunction when in the "Translator's Foreword" to his *Thousand Nights and a Night* he remarks, "Before parting we [a colleague and himself] agreed to 'collaborate' and produce a full, complete, unvarnished, *uncastrated* copy of the great original" (emphasis mine).

10.

وادا ارادت الامراه شيأ لا يقدر احدأ ان يردها. (٦٤)

11.

ها انتم بين يدى السابع من بنى العباس الرشيد ابن المهدى ولد الهادى اخر السفاح بن منصور، فافصحى لسانك وتبتى جنانك، ولا تخبرى الا حقأ وقولى صدقأ، وتجنبى الكدب وعليك بالصدق ولو ان الصدق يحرقك بنار الوعيد (٢٠١)

12.

ثم انه اخدها وعراها وشبحها بين اربع سكك واخد فى عقوبتها وتقريرها... فنظرت الى الصبيه وهى

عريانه مشبوحه والدما يسيل من اجنابها ... ثم انه اخد السيف وضربها طير يدها من مفصلها وضرب
يدها الاخرى طيرها (٤_١٦١)

13.

ثم ان الخليفه ـ ايها الملك ـ احضر ولده الامين بين يديه واستخبره عن القضيب على صحتها. (٢١٨)

14. I have benefited greatly from the fascinating discussion of the significance of numbers in the *1001 Nights* in Ghazoul, *The Arabian Nights*, pp. 62–65. She addresses the issue of the number 1001 on p. 65.

Chapter Six

1. There are indications other than this historical one of the presence of Islam in the story. The ifrit who magically returns the black bitches to their former state is particularly identified as a believer; and the sole survivor in the petrified city of the eldest lady's tale has survived only because of his belief in Allah and his devotion to the practices of Islam. Though none of these instances is insistent, they serve to inform the general background of the cycle.

2. Brooks, "Freud's Masterplot," p. 292. I would disagree with Brooks's statement that "the straight line, the shortest distance between beginning and end . . . would be the collapse of one into the other, of life into death" (ibid.). The gratuitous line of plot to which Brooks here refers in citing *Tristram Shandy* is not necessary in all narratives; indeed, a work like *Tristram Shandy* or *Jacques le fataliste* is remarkable for the extreme arbitrariness of its narrative line, although such digression or transgression can be remarked to varying degrees in all narratives. The narrative line of the comic strip, however, allows for no such detour; nor does that traced by hieroglyphs. In short, it is possible for a narrative to follow a straight line, a direct route, and still retain its status as a narrative as long as there is at least a minimal distance traveled between beginning and end.

3. All definitions are drawn from the most recent edition of the *Oxford English Dictionary*. The example given for the definition meaning Arabian or Arabic is an 1842 statement from the *Encyclopaedia Britannica*: "The inglorious obscurity in which the Arabesque doctors have generally slumbered." Dickens's phrase in

Dombey and Sons (1848), "Surrounded by this arabesque work of his musing fancy . . . ," supports the subsequent definition of "strangely mixed or fantastic."

4. Alois Riegl, quoted by Kühnel in *The Arabesque*, p. 5.

5. Kühnel, *The Arabesque*, p. 16.

6. For discussion of this issue, see the following works, among many: Berque, "A propos de l'art musulman"; Ettinghausen, "Character of Islamic Art"; Ettinghausen, "Early Realism in Islamic Art"; Grabar, *Formation of Islamic Art*.

7. Interestingly enough, the Koran itself offers no such support. Indeed, those who argue for the permissibility of figuration in Islam often cite verses from the Koran as proof. Those most commonly indicated are:

> They made for him, to the extent that
> he desired, sanctuaries and statues.

(XXXIV, 13)

and

> I have come to you with a sign from
> your Lord. I will create for you out of
> clay as the likeness of a bird; then I will
> breathe into it, and it will be a bird
> by the leave of God.

(III, 43)

8. Drawn from Bukhārī's collection of *Ḥadīth*, as quoted by Grabar in *Formation of Islamic Art*, p. 91.

9. Drawn from Bukhārī's collection of *Ḥadīth*, as quoted by Massignon in "Méthodes de réalisation artistique," p. 48.

10. al-Nawawī, as quoted by Arnold in *Painting in Islam*, p. 9. Another *Ḥadīth* collected by Bukhārī is here pertinent: "Who is more wicked than a man who sets to work to imitate the creative activity of God? Let them try to create a grain of wheat, or create an ant."

11. Ibn Sīnā in *Kitāb al-Shiʿr*, as quoted by Cantarino in *Arabic Poetics in the Golden Age*, p. 133.

Bibliography

Literary Theory

Aristotle. *Poetics*. Translated by Ingram Bywater. New York, 1954.

——. *Rhetoric*. Translated by W. Rhys Roberts. New York, 1954.

Assoun, Paul-Laurent. "Pour une histoire philosophique de la répétition." *Corps écrits* 15 (1985): 75–87.

Barthes, Roland. "Rhétorique de l'image." *Communications* 4 (1964): 40–51.

——. "Eléments de sémiologie." *Communications* 4 (1964): 91–134.

——. "Introduction à l'analyse structurale des récits." In *L'analyse structurale du récit*, pp. 7–33. Collection Points. Paris, 1981.

——. *Le plaisir du texte*. Paris, 1973.

Benjamin, Walter. *Illuminations*. Translated by Harry Zohn. Edited and with an introduction by Hannah Arendt. New York, 1969.

Boas, Franz. *Primitive Art*. Cambridge, Mass., 1927.

Borges, Jorge Luis. *Enquêtes*. Paris, 1957.

Brémond, Claude. "Le message narratif." *Communications* 4 (1964): 4–32.

——. "La logique des possibles narratifs." In *L'analyse structurale du récit*, pp. 66–82. Collection Points. Paris, 1981.

——. "Les bons recompensés et les méchants punis." In *Sémiotique narrative et textuelle*, edited by C. Chabrol, pp. 96–121. Paris, 1973.

Brik, Osip. "Rhythme et syntaxe." In *Théorie de la littérature*, translated and edited by Tzvetan Todorov, pp. 143–53. Paris, 1965.

Brooke-Rose, Christine. *A Grammar of Metaphor*. London, 1958.

Brooks, Peter. "Freud's Masterplot." *Yale French Studies* 55–56 (1977): 280–300.

————. *Reading for the Plot: Design and Intention in Narrative.* New York, 1984.

Brownstein, Marilyn. "Post-modern Language and the Perpetuation of Desire." *Twentieth-Century Literature* 15 (1985): 73–86.

Chatelain, Daniele. "Frontières de l'itératif." *Poétique* 17 (1986): 111–24.

Chklovski, Viktor. "L'art comme procédé." In *Théorie de la littérature,* translated and edited by Tzvetan Todorov, pp. 76–98. Paris, 1965.

————. "La construction de la nouvelle et du roman." In *Théorie de la littérature,* translated and edited by Tzvetan Todorov, pp. 170–96. Paris, 1965.

Cohen, Ted. "Metaphor and the Cultivation of Intimacy." In *On Metaphor,* edited by Sheldon Sacks, pp. 1–10. Chicago, 1979.

Dallenbach, Lucien. *Le récit spéculaire.* Paris, 1976.

Deleuze, Gilles. *Différence et répétition.* Paris, 1968.

————. *Logique du sens.* Paris, 1973.

de Man, Paul. "The Epistemology of Metaphor." In *On Metaphor,* edited by Sheldon Sacks, pp. 11–28. Chicago, 1979.

Eikhenbaum, Boris. "Sur la théorie de la prose." In *Théorie de la littérature,* translated and edited by Tzvetan Todorov, pp. 197–211. Paris, 1965.

Erlich, Victor. *Russian Formalism.* 2d ed. The Hague, 1965.

Escal, Françoise. "Ostinato." *Corps écrits* 15 (1985): 45–57.

Foucault, Michel. "Le langage à l'infini." *Tel Quel* 15 (1963): 44–53.

Freud, Sigmund. *Beyond the Pleasure Principle.* Translated by James Strachey. New York, 1961.

————. "The Uncanny." In *Studies in Parapsychology,* edited by Philip Rieff, pp. 19–60. New York, 1963.

Genette, Gérard. "Frontières du récit." In *L'analyse structurale du récit,* pp. 158–69. Collection Points. Paris, 1981.

————. "Le jour, la nuit." *Langages* 12 (1968): 28–42.

————. *Figures III*. Paris, 1972.

————. "L'autre du même." *Corps écrits* 15 (1985): 11–16.

Greimas, A.-J. *Sémantique structurale*. Paris, 1966.

Harries, Karsten. "Metaphor and Transcendence." In *On Metaphor*, edited by Sheldon Sacks, pp. 71–88. Chicago, 1979.

Humphries, Jefferson. "Haunted Words." *Diacritics* 13 (1983): 29–38.

Jakobson, Roman. "Linguistics and Poetics." In *Style in Language*, edited by Thomas Sebeok, pp. 350–77. Cambridge, Mass., 1960.

————. "Du réalisme artistique." In *Théorie de la littérature*, translated and edited by Tzvetan Todorov, pp. 98–108. Paris, 1965.

————. "On Russian Fairy Tales." In *Selected Writings*, vol. 4, pp. 82–100. The Hague, 1966.

————. "Poetry of Grammar and Grammar of Poetry." *Lingua* 21 (1968): 597–609.

————. "Two Aspects of Language and Two Types of Aphasic Disturbances." In *Selected Writings*, vol. 2, pp. 239–59. The Hague, 1971.

————. "Principes de versification." In *Huit questions de poétique*, pp. 40–58. Paris, 1973.

————. *Language in Literature*. Edited by Krystyna Pomorska and Stephen Rudy. Cambridge, Mass., 1988.

Jolles, André. *Formes simples*. Translated by Antoine Buquet. Paris, 1972.

Kawin, Bruce. *Telling It Again and Again*. Ithaca, N.Y., 1972.

Kierkegaard, Søren. *Repetition: An Essay in Experimental Psychology*. Translated by Walter Lowrie. Princeton, N.J., 1946.

Lawlor, Leonard. "Event and Repeatability: Ricoeur and Derrida in Debate." *Pre/Text* 4 (1983): 317–34.

Lefebve, Maurice-Jean. *Structure du discours de la poésie et du récit*. Neufchâtel, 1971.

Lévi-Strauss, Claude. "The Structural Study of Myth." *Journal of American Folklore* 68 (1955): 428–44.

Lord, Albert. *The Singer of Tales.* Cambridge, Mass., 1960.

Miller, J. Hillis. *Fiction and Repetition: Seven English Novels.* Cambridge, Mass., 1982.

Mukarovsky, Jan. "Standard Language and Poetic Language." In *A Prague School Reader on Esthetics, Literary Structure, and Style,* translated by P. Garvin, pp. 17–30. Washington, D.C., 1964.

Prince, Gerald. *A Grammar of Stories: An Introduction.* The Hague, 1973.

Propp, Vladimir. *Morphology of the Folk-Tale.* Translated by Laurence Scott. 2d ed. Austin, Tex., 1968.

Ricoeur, Paul. "The Metaphorical Process as Cognition, Imagination, and Feeling." In *On Metaphor,* edited by Sheldon Sacks, pp. 141–57. Chicago, 1979.

Rimmon-Kenan, Shlomith. "The Paradoxical Status of Repetition." *Poetics Today* 1 (1980): 151–59.

Said, Edward. *Beginnings: Intention and Method.* New York, 1975.

———. *Orientalism.* New York, 1976.

———. *The World, the Text, and the Critic.* Cambridge, Mass., 1985.

Suleiman, Susan. *Authoritarian Fictions: The Ideological Novel as a Literary Genre.* New York, 1983.

Todorov, Tzvetan. "Les catégories du récit littéraire." In *L'analyse structurale du récit,* pp. 131–57. Collection Points. Paris, 1981.

———. "La grammaire du récit." *Langages* 12 (1968): 94–102.

———. *Grammaire du Décameron.* The Hague, 1969.

———. "La quête du récit." In *Poétique de la prose,* pp. 59–80. Collection Points. Paris, 1978.

———. "Les transformations narratives." *Poétique* 3 (1970): 322–33.

———. *Poétique de la prose.* Collection Points. Paris, 1978.

Urbye, Renée. "La texture de l'énoncé littéraire." *Revue romane* 18 (1979): 111–27.

Zumthor, Paul. *Essai de poétique mediévale.* Paris, 1972.

Arabic Literature and Poetics

Editions of the 1001 Nights

The Alif Laila or the Book of the Thousand Nights and One Night, Commonly Known as "The Arabian Nights Entertainment," now for the first time published complete in the original Arabic, from an Egyptian Manuscript brought to India by the late Major Turner, editor of the Shah-Nameh. Edited by W. H. Macnaghten, Esq. 4 vols. Calcutta, 1839–42.

The Arabian Nights Entertainment; In the Original Arabic, published under the Patronage of the College of Fort William. Edited by Shuekh Uhmud bin Moohummud Shirwanee ul Yumunee. 2 vols. Calcutta, 1814, 1818.

Kitāb Alf Laylah wa-Laylah. Edited by ʿAbd al-Raḥmān al-Ṣafatī al-Sharqāwī. 2 vols. Bulaq, Cairo, 1835.

Tausend und eine Nacht: Arabisch, nach eine Handschrift aus Tunis. Edited by Maximilian Habicht. 12 vols. Breslau, 1824–43.

The 1001 Nights (Alf Layla wa-Layla) from the Earliest Known Sources. Edited and with an introduction by Muhsin Mahdi. Leiden, 1984.

Other Works

Abdel-Meguid, Abdel-Aziz. "A Survey of Short Literature in Arabic from before Islam to the Middle of the Nineteenth Century." *Islamic Quarterly* 1 (1954): 104–12.

Abounader, M. "Le conte dans les *Mille et une nuits:* Essai d'analyse sémiotique." Ph.D. diss., Paris, 1973.

Abu Deeb, Kamal. "al-Jurjānī's Classification of Istiʿāra with Special Reference to Aristotle's Classification of Metaphor." *Journal of Arabic Literature* 2 (1971): 48–75.

———. *al-Jurjānī's Theory of Poetic Imagery.* Warminster, 1979.

Ali, Muhsin Jassim. "The Arabian Nights in Eighteenth-Century English Criticism." *Muslim World* 67 (1977): 12–32.

al-ʿAskarī. *Kitāb al-Ṣināʿatayn.* Edited by Alī Bajawī and Muḥammad Ibrahīm. Cairo, 1971.

Beeston, A. F. L. "Parallelism in Arabic Prose." *Journal of Arabic Literature* 5 (1974): 134–46.

Bellamy, James. "Sex and Society in Islamic Popular Literature." In *Society and the Sexes,* edited by Afaf Lutfi al-Sayyid-Marsot, pp. 23–42. Malibu, Calif., 1979.

Bencheikh, Jamaleddine. "Premières propositions pour une théorie d'un schéma générateur: Essai d'analyse du texte narratif dans un conte des *1001 nuits.*" *Théories/Analyses: Etudes arabes travaux Vincennes* 1 (1981): 136–89.

Bencheneb, Rachid. "Les *1001 nuits* et le théâtre arabe au vingtième siècle." *Studia Islamica* 45 (1977): 101–37.

Bodine, J. J. "Magic Carpet to Islam: Duncan Black Macdonald and the Arabian Nights." *Muslim World* 67 (1977): 1–11.

Borges, Jorge Luis. "The Thousand and One Nights." In *Seven Nights,* translated by Eliot Weinberger, pp. 42–57. New York, 1984.

Boullata, Issa. "Verbal Arabesque and Mystical Union: A Study of Ibn al-Farid's al-Ta'iyya al-Kubra." *Arab Studies Quarterly* 3 (1981): 152–69.

Brockway, D. "The Macdonald Collection of Arabian Nights: A Bibliography." *Muslim World* 61 (1971): 256–66; 63 (1973): 185–203; 64 (1974): 16–32.

Burgel, J. C. "Love, Lust and Longing: Eroticism in Early Islam as Reflected in Literary Sources." In *Society and the Sexes,* edited by Afaf Lutfi al-Sayyid-Marsot, pp. 81–117. Malibu, Calif., 1979.

Burton, Richard, trans. *The Book of the Thousand Nights and a Night.* 16 vols. N.d.

Cantarino, Vincent. *Arabic Poetics in the Golden Age.* Leiden, 1975.

Chauvin, Vincent. *Bibliography on the "1001 Nights."* In vol. 4 of *Bibliographie des ouvrages arabes ou relatifs aux arabes,* pp. 82–120. Liège: 1892–1907.

Clinton, Jerome. "Madness and Cure in the *1001 Nights.*" In *Fairy Tales and Society: Illusion, Allusion, and Paradigm,* edited by Ruth B. Bottigheimer, pp. 35–51. Philadelphia, 1986.

Dehoi, E. *L'éroticism des "Mille et une nuits."* Paris, 1961.

Drory, R. "Ali Baba and the Forty Thieves: An Attempt at a Model for the Narrative Structure of the Reward and Punishment Fairy Tale." In *Patterns in Oral Literature,* edited by H. Jason and D. Segal, pp. 33–48. The Hague, 1977.

Farag, F. Rafail. "The Arabian Nights, a Mirror of Islam in the Middle Ages." *Arabica* 23 (1976): 197–211.

Faris, Wendy. "1001 Words: Fiction against Death." *Georgia Review* 36 (1982): 811–30.

Gerhardt, Mia. *The Art of Story-Telling: A Literary Study of "The Thousand and One Nights."* Leiden, 1963.

Gerresch, Claude. "Un récit des *1001 nuits:* Tawaddud: Petite encyclopédie de l'Islam mediévale." *Bulletin de l'Institut fondamental de l'Afrique noire* 35 (1973): 57–175.

Ghazi, M. Ferid. "La littérature d'imagination en arabe du II/VIII au V/XI siècle." *Arabica* 4 (1957): 164–78.

Ghazoul, Ferial. *The Arabian Nights: A Structural Analysis.* Cairo, 1980.

———. "The *Arabian Nights* and Shakespearian Comedy: 'The Sleeper Awakened' and the 'Tale of the Shrew.'" In *Mundus Arabicus: Essays on the "1001 Nights,"* pp. 58–70. Cambridge, Mass., 1985.

Grossman, Judith. "Infidelity and Fiction." *Georgia Review* 34, no. 1 (Spring 1980): 113–26.

Grotzfeld, Heinz. "Neglected Conclusions of the Arabian Nights: Gleanings in Forgotten and Overlooked Recensions." *Journal of Arabic Literature* 16 (1985): 73–87.

Grunebaum, Gustave von. *A Tenth Century Document of Arabic Literary Theory and Criticism: The Sections on Poetry of al-Baqillānī's I'jāz al-Qur'ān.* Chicago, 1950.

Haddawy, Husain, trans. *The Arabian Nights.* New York, 1990.

Hageg, Claude. "Traitement du sens et fidelité dans l'adaptation classique: Sur le texte arabe des *Mille et une nuits* et la traduction de Galland." *Arabica* 27 (1980): 114–39.

Hamori, Andras. *On the Art of Medieval Arabic Literature.* Princeton, N.J., 1974.

———. "Notes on Two Love Stories from the *1001 Nights.*" *Studia Islamica* 43 (1976): 65–80.

———. "A Comic Romance from the *1001 Nights:* The Tale of the Two Viziers." *Arabica* 30 (1983): 38–56.

———. "The Magician and the Whore: Readings of *Qamar al-*

Zaman." In *Mundus Arabicus: Essays on the "1001 Nights,"* pp. 25–57. Cambridge, Mass., 1985.

Hawari, Rida. "Antoine Galland's Translation of the *Arabian Nights.*" *Revue de la littérature comparée* 54 (1980): 150–64.

Heath, Peter. "Romance as Genre in 'The Thousand and One Nights.'" Parts 1, 2. *Journal of Arabic Literature* 18, 19 (1989): 1–21; 1–26.

Heinrichs, Wolfhart. *The Hand of the North-Wind: Opinions on Metaphor and the Early Meaning of Isti'āra in Arabic Poetics.* Wiesbaden, 1977.

Keyser, James. "The *1001 Nights:* A Famous Etiquette Book." *Edebiyat* 3 (1978): 11–22.

Knipp, C. "The *Arabian Nights* in England: Galland's Translation and Its Successors." *Journal of Arabic Literature* 5 (1974): 44–54.

al-Jurjānī, 'Abd al-Qāhir. *Asrār al-Balāghah.* Edited by H. Ritter. Istanbul, 1954.

Littmann, E. "Alf-Layla wa-Layla." In *The Encyclopedia of Islam.* 2d ed.

Macdonald, Duncan Black. "Maximilian Habicht and His Recension of the *1001 Nights.*" *Journal of the Royal Asiatic Society,* 1909, pp. 685–704.

———. "Lost MS of the *Arabian Nights* and a Projected Edition of that of Galland." *Journal of the Royal Asiatic Society,* 1911, pp. 219–26.

———. "From the *Arabian Nights* to Spirit." *Moslem World* 9 (1919): 336–48.

———. "The Earlier History of the *Arabian Nights.*" *Journal of the Royal Asiatic Society,* 1924, pp. 353–97.

———. "One Thousand and One Nights." In *Encyclopaedia Britannica.* 14th ed.

———. "A Bibliographical and Literary Study of the First Appearance of the *Arabian Nights* in Europe." *Library Quarterly* 2 (1932): 387–42.

Mahdi, Muhsin. "Maẓāhir al-Riwāyah wa-al-Mushāfaha fī Uṣūl 'Alf Laylah wa-Laylah.'" *Revue de l'Institut des manuscrits arabes* 20 (March 1974): 125–44.

———. "Exemplary Tales in the *1001 Nights.*" In *Mundus Arabicus: Essays on the "1001 Nights,"* pp. 1–24. Cambridge, Mass., 1985.

Matarasso, Michel. "In Praise of Double Sexuality in the *1001 Nights.*" *Diogenes* 118 (1982): 12–48.

Miquel, André. *Ajib et Gharib: Un conte des "Mille et une nuits."* Paris, 1978.

———. "Mille nuits plus une." *Critique* 394 (March 1980): 241–46.

———. "Dossier d'un conte des *Mille et une nuits.*" *Critique* 394 (March 1980): 274–77.

———. *Sept contes des "Mille et une nuits."* Paris, 1981.

Molan, Peter. "Maʿruf the Cobbler: The Mythic Structure of an *Arabian Nights* Tale." *Edebiyat* 3 (1978): 121–35.

———. "Sindbad the Sailor: A Commentary on the Ethics of Violence." *Journal of African and Oriental Studies* 98 (1978): 237–47.

Moussa-Mahmoud, Fatma. "A MS Translation of the *Arabian Nights* in the Beckford Papers." *Journal of Arabic Literature* (1976): 7–23.

Murphy, Christopher M. "A Brief Look at Illustrated Translations of the *Arabian Nights.*" In *Mundus Arabicus: Essays on the "1001 Nights,"* pp. 86–100. Cambridge, Mass., 1985.

Pellat, Charles. "Kinaya." In *The Encyclopedia of Islam.* 2d ed.

Perès, Henri. "Le roman dans la littérature arabe des origines à la fin du moyen âge." *Annales de l'Institut d'études orientales* 16 (1958): 5–40.

Rosenthal, Franz. "Fiction and Reality: Sources for the Role of Sex in Medieval Muslim Society." In *Society and the Sexes,* edited by Afaf Lutfi al-Sayyid-Marsot, pp. 3–22. Malibu, Calif., 1979.

al-Thaʿālibī, Abū Manṣūr ʿAbd al-Malik ibn Muḥammad. *Kitāb Kināyah wa-al-Taʿrīḍ.* Cairo, 1908.

Todorov, Tzvetan. "Les hommes-récits." In *Poétique de la prose,* pp. 33–46. Collection Points. Paris, 1978.

Trilton, A.-S. "Folklore in Arabic Literature." *Folklore* 60 (1949): 332–53.

Walters, J. R. "Michel Butor and the *1001 Nights.*" *Neophilologus* 59 (1975): 213–22.

Weber, Edgar. "Situation initiale et situation finale dans quelques contes des *Mille et une nuits.*" *Littérature* 11 (1984): 65–73.

Wright, M. *A Grammar of the Arabic Language.* 3d ed. Cambridge, 1971.

Islamic Arts and Aesthetics

Ardalan, Nader, and Laleh Bakhtiar. *The Sense of Unity: The Sufi Tradition in Persian Architecture.* Chicago, 1973.

Arnold, T. W. *Painting in Islam.* Oxford, 1928.

Aziza, M. *Calligraphie arabe.* Tunis, 1973.

———. *L'image et l'Islam.* Paris, 1978.

Berque, Jacques. "A propos de l'art musulman: Remarques sur le non-figuratif." In *Normes et valeurs dans l'Islam contemporain,* edited by Jean-Paul Charnay, pp. 101–13. Paris, 1966.

———. "Sur un motif ornemental." In *Mélanges Taha Hussein,* edited by Abdurrahman Badawi, pp. 7–15. Cairo, 1962.

Creswell, K. A. C. "The Lawfulness of Painting in Early Islam." *Islamic Culture* 24 (1950): 218–25.

Ettinghausen, Richard. "The Character of Islamic Art." In *The Arab Heritage,* edited by N. A. Faris, pp. 251–67. Princeton, N.J., 1944.

———. "Early Realism in Islamic Art." In *Studii orientalistici in onore G. Della Vida,* vol. 1, pp. 250–73. Rome, 1956.

Farès, Bishr. *Essai sur l'esprit de la décoration islamique.* Cairo, 1952.

———. "Philosophie et jurisprudence illustrées par les arabes: La querelle des images en Islam." In *Mélanges Louis Massignon,* vol. 2, pp. 77–109. Damascus, 1957.

Grabar, Oleg. *The Formation of Islamic Art.* New Haven, Conn., 1973.

Grunebaum, Gustave von. "Idéologie musulmane et esthétique arabe." *Studia Islamica* 3 (1955): 5–24.

———. "Byzantine Iconoclasm and the Influence of the Islamic Environment." *History of Religions* 2 (1962): 1–10.

Hodgson, M. G. S. "Islam and Image." *History of Religions* 3 (1964): 220–60.

Joseph, Roger. "The Semiotics of the Islamic Mosque." *Arab Studies Quarterly* 3 (1981): 285–96.

Khatibi, 'Abd al-Kabir. *La blessure du nom propre.* Paris, 1974.

———. *L'art calligraphique arabe.* Paris, 1976.

Kühnel, E. *The Arabesque: Meaning and Transformation of an Ornament.* Graz, 1976.

Landau, Ron. *The Arabesque: The Abstract Art of Islam.* San Francisco, 1955.

Marcais, Georges. "La question des images dans l'art musulman." *Byzantion* 7 (1932): 161–83.

———. "L'arabesque: vocabulaire et esthétique." *Annuaire de l'Institut de philologie et d'histoire orientales* 13 (1953): 323–30.

Mason, J. P. "Structural Congruities in the Arab Genealogical Form and the Arabesque Motif." *Muslim World* 65 (1975): 21–33.

Massignon, Louis. "Les méthodes de réalisation artistique des peuples de l'Islam." *Revue Syria* 2 (1921): 47–53, 149–60.

el-Said, Issam, and Aysa Parman. *Geometric Concepts in Islamic Art.* London, 1975.

Sandler, R. "Islamic Art: Variations on Themes of Arabesque." In *Introduction to Islamic Civilisation,* edited by R. M. Savory, pp. 89–109. Cambridge, 1976.

Index

Index

West, the, translation of *1001 Nights* from the East to, 4, 6

Woman/women, 9; appropriation of power in *1001 Nights*, 99–103; inclusion in catalog of ugly things, 26; as narrator of *1001 Nights*, 5, 7, 14; saved from ex-

tinction by the narrator of *1001 Nights*, 14. *See also* Feminine, the/Feminine realm; Voice, women's

Word(s): connection with thing, 19, 21, 22, 25, 47; euphemisms used for, 26